Breaking the Fifth Wall:

Rethinking Arts Marketing for the 21st Century

Eugene Carr

Michelle Paul

Patron Publishing
A division of Patron Technology, LLC
850 Seventh Avenue, Suite 1201
New York, NY 10019

Cover design by Harriet Goren
Cover photo by Ma'ayan Plaut
Back cover photos by Suzanne Sheridan and Daniella Zalcman
Text layout by Michelle Kettner

Library of Congress Control Number: 2011922847
ISBN: 978-0-9729141-6-1

First Printing February 2011

Printed in the United States of America

Eugene Carr, founder and CEO of Patron Technology, has been an innovator in the area of e-marketing for arts & cultural organizations since 1996, when he founded CultureFinder.com, which became an award-winning nationwide arts calendar and online ticketing service.

Gene earned a BA in History from Oberlin College, and a music degree from Oberlin Conservatory, earning Phi Kappa Lambda honors, and then earned an MBA from Columbia Business School. After receiving his MBA, he worked in Gold and Platinum Card marketing at American Express. Gene worked in arts management serving as the executive director of the American Symphony Orchestra from 1991-1996, while serving in the same role for the Concordia Orchestra.

Gene is the author of three previous books on e-marketing: *Wired for Culture: How E-mail is Revolutionizing Arts Marketing* (Third Edition) (2007), *Sign-Up for Culture: The Arts Marketer's Guide to Building an Effective E-mail List* (Second Edition) (2007), and *Web Sites for Culture: Essential Principles for Great Arts Web Sites* (2005).

Michelle Paul, Director of Product Development, has been in charge of building and improving PatronManager CRM since its conceptualization and launch. She works closely with the client base to come up with new features and help them get the most out of the system.

A close observer of arts marketing and management trends, Michelle has been giving seminars on the topic since 2008, including multi-city tours in the United States and Spain.

Michelle is on the board of ELNYA (Emerging Leaders of New York Arts), a professional development group for arts administrators in their 20s and 30s. She holds a B.A. in Classics from Wesleyan University, but spends much more time dealing with apex code exceptions than translating ancient Greek, these days.

Patron Technology aims to revolutionize the business of the arts and other live events by offering world-class customer relationship management (CRM) technology, including box office ticketing, fundraising, e-mail marketing, and staff collaboration, all in one system. Patron Technology's products, PatronManager CRM and PatronMail are used by over 1,500 organizations worldwide.

Acknowledgements

This book has been a project of nearly two years, and we want to acknowledge the people who have helped guide its development during this time.

First, our main editor, Eric Zakim, Associate Professor at the School of Languages, Literatures, and Cultures, University of Maryland, immeasurably sharpened and focused our thinking and writing.

We got terrific comments from a range of friends and colleagues, and offer our thanks to the following industry experts: Thomas Cott, Director of Marketing, Alvin Ailey Dance Foundation; Nathan Newbrough, President/CEO, Colorado Springs Philharmonic; Wende Persons, Consultant, Steven Roth, President, The Pricing Institute and Board Chair, ArtsBoston; David Snead, Vice President of Marketing, New York Philharmonic.

We also benefited from feedback and insight from our friends and from members of the Patron Technology staff: Nathan Anderson, Lorna Dolci, Megan Gendell, Dael Norwood, and Lily Traub.

Because our own focus-group studies and web-based surveys are a central part of the early chapters, we have relied on the expert guidance of Steve Brock of BlueBear, LLC in Cincinnati, and Ariel Fishman, Director of Institutional Research at Yeshiva University.

Thanks to all.

-EVC & MP

TABLE OF CONTENTS

SECTION I: Introduction

Chapter 1

Breaking the Fifth Wall

As any actor will tell you, the Fourth Wall refers to the imaginary separation in a theatre between the action on stage and the audience sitting in the dark watching the play. When an actor "breaks the Fourth Wall," he turns and speaks directly to the audience, breaking the illusion of the autonomy of the action. The effect is often startling—even a bit jarring—as the imaginary world of the stage is momentarily interrupted.

And when the play or concert is over, the audience passes through another wall: the "Fifth Wall" that separates the cultural experience (and the organization that produced it) from the ongoing life of the audience member. This effect can be equally jarring, as the lights come up and the world of the arts experience fades before the real world of parking lots, bad weather, and the late-night news.

The Fifth Wall separates your patrons both physically and mentally from your organization. Breaking the Fifth Wall is the act of reconnecting with those patrons in a meaningful way *after* they have left your venue, by creatively and regularly reminding them of the value of the arts experience your organization offers, coaxing them to return, and perhaps ultimately convincing them to donate. In the past, you might have simply called this "marketing," but today, what's required is more accurately described as "patron relationship building."

The world has changed, and so too has the audience. The way arts marketers have gone about building relationships with audiences over the last fifty years is no longer relevant, and no longer works.

Subscription brochures, newspaper ads, and telemarketing calls are not enough anymore to connect to your audience and keep them coming back. The old "butts in seats" paradigm is simply too crude to be an effective goal in this more complex world. Of course, you want to fill your seats. But to address what's truly ailing arts marketing, you must refocus on a set of new and different goals, and transform your organization's audience-development efforts.

This book proposes an entirely new framework for arts marketing as we begin the second decade of the 21st century. The arts-going experience is ultimately about a connection between the artist and the audience. Now, because of advances in technology and changes in consumer behavior, the arts experience—*and arts marketing as well*—is evolving into an interactive relationship that reaches far beyond a physical venue. It's time to discard the "what we've always done" thinking that permeates the industry, and take a new approach that will lead to deeper and more meaningful patron relationships. This approach is what we call breaking the Fifth Wall.

How the World Has Changed

The way arts patrons access information about events and make the decision to attend them has evolved more in the past decade than it had since the invention of the radio or television. These changes are not superficial—they alter the landscape that arts managers must operate in.

- Arts audiences are now living online. As the Internet has become ubiquitous, it's no longer a question of *whether* your audience can be reached online. The question is, *how, when,* and *where* is it most effective to do so?

- Old media—particularly print newspapers and magazines—are in steep decline, and their audiences are rapidly migrating to the Internet. What we used to call "new media" are no longer new anymore.

• A substantial portion of arts patrons prefer e-mail over direct mail communications from their favorite arts organizations. *Wired for Culture: How E-mail is Revolutionizing Arts Marketing*, first published in 2003, suggested that if your patrons signed up for your e-mail list, and if you sent them regular, relevant, compelling, engaging, and useful information, they would respond in dramatic numbers. Today, we *know* this to be true. E-mail marketing works. Response rates for e-mail campaigns are much higher than for direct mail, and the cost to send e-mail is dramatically lower.

• As ticket sales move to the Internet, arts websites have become the most important public face of an organization. In many cases, they have become the point of sale for more than a third of all tickets arts organizations sell each year, superseding the box office and the telephone. Some organizations sell almost 70 percent of their tickets online![1] A poorly designed website, or one that is nothing more than an online version of the season brochure, can cause great damage to the image of the organization.

• The subscription, once the central and most reliable relationship an arts organization had with its core audience, an idea codified thirty years ago in the seminal volume *Subscribe Now*, by Danny Newman, is under siege. The fixed annual series is being replaced by the make-your-own series, flexible subscription packages, and more last-minute single-ticket sales than ever before. This transformation has led to a dramatic reduction in upfront cash and an unrelenting need to market empty seats until the very last minute.

• Social media has arrived, and it is not going away. What seemed like a fad only a few years ago has evolved into a worldwide phenomenon, with Facebook and Twitter leading the way. Today, if arts managers ignore social media, they do so at their own peril.

Arts Marketing Challenges and Opportunities

For years, online marketing was treated as an afterthought to an organization's core marketing program. Marketers initially saw the Internet as simply another "place" to promote their organizations. The first online marketing strategies were simplistic efforts that mirrored offline approaches and objectives.

While many arts marketers were ignoring the stunning potential of the Internet, the online world continued to evolve, and the number of touch points to connect with patrons increased dramatically. You can now reach them on their computers, smartphones, and iPads. You can e-mail them, tweet at them, "push" news to them, and chat with them on social media sites. The online world has become a multifaceted and complex patchwork of overlapping technologies, and e-marketing can no longer be boiled down to one simple approach, let alone an approach that mimics the techniques from the old print world.

The good news about the Internet's complexity is that the cost to reach patrons has decreased, since digital marketing is fundamentally less expensive than offline marketing. In the analog world, most marketing efforts were one-time, blind do-or-die propositions. You sent out direct mail, placed newspaper and radio ads, and hoped for the best. All of this had to be done with extreme care, because you were making a significant investment on pulling a mailing list, printing and postage, deciding on your message, and writing the copy. If you didn't get it just right, not only did it cost you dearly, but you had to wait until the next season to try again.

On the other hand, you can test digital marketing approaches instantly and inexpensively to find out what works before committing your entire budget to a single approach.

In arts marketing, the scarce resource isn't money anymore—it's your audience's *attention*. With the increase in touch points comes a decrease in time spent with any one of them. The average time a user spends on a website is measured in minutes, and time on e-mail in only seconds. Twitter offers just 140 characters per message. With so many new ways to reach arts patrons—and with less time spent on each—your marketing efforts need to be concise, thought out, and well executed if you want to attract your patrons' attention.

What all this means is that the old ways of developing and maintaining a relationship with your audience are antiquated and much less effective than they used to be. You've got to embrace and adopt new rules, new technologies, and new approaches that squarely address the changed audience and the changed marketing environment you're working in.

Success will come when you connect to today's arts patrons in the way they *want to be reached*. Then, you need to *manage these relationships* in the most efficient and effective way possible in order to maintain their interest and keep them coming back.

The Age of Customer Relationship Management

Customer Relationship Management (CRM) systems are the most important arts management technologies to come along in the last fifty years. CRM starts with the fundamental proposition that the best way to build a relationship with a customer is to put her at the center of your marketing world by compiling and displaying all of her information and transactions in one place, on one technology platform that is accessible and constantly updated by all employees of your organization.

For too long, you've had your customer data spread out across different departments in your organization. Your staff could not see a patron's entire history in one place. You might know a lot about her, but you couldn't get a 360-degree picture. If your information is dispersed among various databases in your office, you cannot understand your patron as a real person with distinct needs, interests, and priorities.

A CRM system will simplify the management of your data—both current and historical—by integrating all of your organization's information and databases into a single, seamless unit.

Once you have all your patron data in a single database, and that information is accessible online to *everyone in your organization*, then your organization can make dramatic improvements in efficiency, customer service, and marketing effectiveness. CRM is not simply a fancy name for a new ticketing or fundraising system—it's a system that enables an entirely new paradigm for how to run your organization.

In the decade to come, CRM promises to spur a complete transformation of the back-office operations of arts and cultural organizations. This technology is several magnitudes more powerful and several magnitudes less expensive than anything the vast majority of arts managers have had at their disposal in the past. CRM will offer arts managers an opportunity to break the Fifth Wall and build long-standing one-to-one relationships with their patrons, ones that will extend far beyond the boundaries of their own venues.

The Age of Social Media

Social media helps you to break the Fifth Wall by enabling you to have a direct relationship with individual patrons and communities of patrons in a public arena. The first widely successful social media sites, Facebook and Twitter, offer a new and profoundly different platform for people to communicate with each other. These social media sites are transforming the ability of organizations to engage groups of like-minded people. Social media goes beyond mass marketing by cutting out the middleman, breaking the Fifth Wall, and turning your marketing message into something personal.

Some of you may not yet be convinced of the importance and effectiveness of social media. However, we all agree that no matter how effective your paid marketing efforts are, the hands-down winner for driving people to attend and participate in all things cultural has always been—and will continue to be—*word of mouth*.

In many ways, social media is simply word of mouth on steroids. If you can both initiate and participate in discussions that other people are having about your organization and your art, you can harness word of mouth as a real marketing tool. Social media allows you to do just that.

It's always fascinating to read stories in *The New York Times* about a Broadway show about to close. The writer will often sum up by saying that the show "never found its audience." That's just code for the fact that despite a huge marketing effort, people simply didn't like the show enough to talk it up to their friends.

A friend telling another about what you're doing is far more effective than any statement you can make on your own behalf. Word of mouth is the *sine qua non* of arts marketing, and it's as true today as it was fifty years ago. The only difference is that today, the Internet enables you to make it work for you in an entirely new way.

Social media is so new and profoundly transformative that it challenges traditional definitions of marketing. And because social media sites are new and ever-changing, their rules of engagement can confound even the savviest and most experienced marketer. But with the proper approach, you can use social media to dramatically change the way you establish connections with your patrons.

Why We Wrote This Book

Patron Technology is a mission-oriented software company whose goal is to leverage the power of the Internet to help build arts audiences and interest in the arts in our society. This book, published by Patron Technology, aims to fulfill part of that mission by helping arts managers understand and embrace new technologies and new thinking.

All of this started back in 1995, when Gene Carr won an entrepreneurship competition sponsored by AOL and created CultureFinder.com, an online arts portal. During the heyday of the first dot-com boom, he realized that e-mail was the most important online marketing tool for the arts, not websites.

As a result, in 2001, Gene founded Patron Technology and led the shift to e-mail marketing in the arts field. Today, over 1,800 arts and culture and non-profit organizations in all fifty states and eight countries use the PatronMail® e-mail marketing system to manage their e-mail campaigns. All together, these clients send over 25 million e-mail messages every month. Because of our experience, we believe we have a unique understanding of how arts patrons respond to e-marketing.

Michelle Paul joined Patron Technology in 2005, and her role has been to develop new products and services, with a focus on CRM and social media. She oversees the product development of PatronManager CRM®, and manages the company's educational seminar programming about e-marketing of all kinds.

Our experience does not come from our clients alone. We've used an off-the-shelf CRM system, Salesforce CRM, to run our business since the day the company started. That has played a big part in convincing us that CRM is the future. Now, we've partnered with salesforce. com and the Salesforce Foundation to develop our own product, PatronManager CRM, for the arts and non-profit industry. It's a software system that combines ticketing, subscriptions, e-mail marketing, donor development, day-to-day task management, and calendars—designed to meet the needs of arts organizations of all sizes.

When we started writing this book, we thought it would be enough to revise and update the three previous books Gene has written: *Wired for Culture*, *Sign-Up for Culture*, and *Web Sites for Culture*. It wasn't long before we realized that we needed to do much more than that. The world has changed so fundamentally in even the four years since the last edition of *Wired for Culture* that we decided to write this completely new volume, which is based on the premise that the arts now require an entirely new approach to audience development.

How to Use This Book

While you may decide to read this book straight through from cover to cover, it's been written as a series of five discrete lessons divided into the most important areas you need to focus on to be successful in the 21st century and break the Fifth Wall.

In Section I, we take stock of the *online arts patron*. Who is she? What does she do? We will present research from our own nationwide survey of arts patrons. This will help you understand better who your online patrons are, how they behave online, and how they interact with arts organizations.

Then, in Section II, we turn to *e-mail marketing*, which should be the bedrock of your digital marketing strategy. E-mail is the most powerful online marketing tool you have, and though it's not as new or exciting as some of the other things we discuss, it's still the most important.

Your *website* is the public face of your organization, but how well does it represent you? In Section III, we present the focus-group research Patron Technology conducted with arts patrons, which found out that most arts websites could be greatly improved with a few simple but powerful design guidelines. And *ticketing*, the most important e-commerce function on your site, has its own rules, which we put under a microscope.

In Section IV, Michelle defines what makes *social media* work in the arts. She will provide you with solid tips and techniques for building and strengthening patron relationships using Facebook and Twitter.

In Section V, we focus on CRM and explain in detail just how revolutionary a change it can be, and how *cloud computing* makes CRM possible and affordable.

At the conclusion, in Section VI, Gene augurs some *predictions* about the future by analyzing the trends and technologies that are likely to create new opportunities for arts management in the years to come.

Our objective is to help you understand the world your patrons are living in, and show you how to reach them. We will introduce the most important technologies that are currently emerging, and offer sensible, actionable, and affordable ways to leverage them.

Before we go further, we want to emphasize that we are mindful that most arts organizations operate on slim budgets and have small staffs. As such, nothing in this book requires a large budget or capital investment. We have tried to present good strategies and effective tactics that can benefit organizations of any size.

As we enter the second decade of the 21st century, we believe that in many ways the golden age of non-profit cultural marketing is just beginning. This is an exciting time for rethinking our industry by examining the ways technology can advance the arts. Now, let's get started breaking that Fifth Wall!

Chapter 2

The Online Arts Patron Today

The arts industry is small compared with other entertainment and leisure industries, and there are few commercial research companies that report on the economic trends within it. That's why in each of the last six years, Patron Technology has fielded a nationwide arts patron tracking study with the goal of understanding the behavior and thinking of the online arts consumer, and increasing the collective knowledge of the field.

In our studies, we invite ten to fifteen of our PatronMail clients to distribute via e-mail an online marketing research survey to their patrons. We select the organizations across arts genres (theatre, music, opera, dance, and museums) and balance the geographic reach of the survey across the U.S., reaching both concentrated urban centers and smaller cities across the country. Each organization receives the data of its own patrons, and we aggregate the responses across all the organizations to get our national results. In 2010, we expanded the study to 23 organizations (listed in Appendix A). We sent out 183,000 surveys, and got a 6-percent response rate, receiving back more than 10,000 responses.

For the sake of clarity, and to help you as you review these results, we want to emphasize that the data we report here are not meant to represent the arts-going public as a whole. By only researching the segment of the audience that could be reached through their *participation in opt-in arts e-mail lists*, the data will necessarily be skewed towards those who are already online and who are responding to online marketing.

The value in examining this audience is that as you will see, these online patrons look strikingly similar to the rest of your audience in terms of their demographics. And looking at the trends of the last several years, it's likely that the online participation of your audience will only increase as the quality of the online experience continues to improve and as the gadgets that people use to access the Internet become more like any other easily accessed consumer device.

Thus, examining this online-centered audience gives you a window into an increasingly representative portion of your entire audience base. This is not to say that there are not holdouts in your audience—a segment of people who are not, and will never be Internet-focused. This survey doesn't represent them, and this book isn't about them. But we believe that this "non-digital" portion of your audience, no matter how large it is today, will very likely become smaller and smaller as we move into the future.

Rather than publishing the detailed survey results with pages of charts and graphs, we've summarized our findings into the seven major trends that emerged when we analyzed the data.

Here are our findings.

1. Arts-audience demographics are very narrow

Our data confirm what you probably already know about the age of arts audiences—they are older. Two thirds of respondents are women, and nearly half are over the age of 55. Only 13 percent are under the age of 35. Though some arts genres attract consistently younger audiences (new music, dance, and contemporary theatre, for instance), the overall demographics of our survey are representative of the arts audience as a whole.

Our findings also show that older audience members are online in a significant way. About 90 percent of all patrons said they go online at least once a day, and over 70 percent are online at least twice a day. Even if we focus only on patrons over age 55, we find that about 87 percent spend at least one hour a day online.

On average, how frequently do you use the Internet?

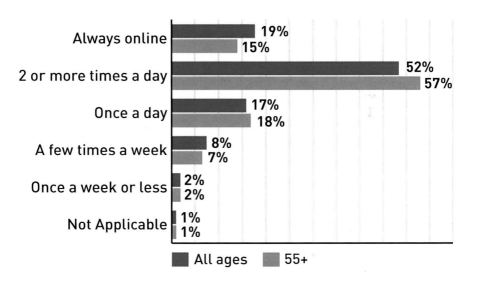

As you would also expect, the arts audience is highly educated. Half of the respondents have graduate degrees, and another 33 percent have at least a bachelor's degree. By comparison, only 9 percent of the general population in the United States has graduate degrees.[2]

The average household income of this group is also high. Even though a third of respondents chose not to answer the question, 57 percent of those who did fell in the $50,000–$150,000 income range.

These demographics should seem familiar to you. Highly educated, mostly female, older, with a high average household income: that probably mirrors the audience you already know. These online arts patrons can serve as an analogue for your audience as a whole.

2. Newspapers' influence continues to decline

For the past few decades, daily print newspapers had been the most stable and consistent advertising vehicle for arts managers to quickly and efficiently promote their events. But by now we all know how challenged the newspaper industry is, which has significant implications for the arts. Our survey data reflect a dramatic change in consumer behavior and attitudes toward newspapers.

We asked patrons to select the degree to which newspapers were a source of information driving their arts attendance. As was to be expected, positive responses declined significantly from 2007 to 2010. When we asked how much patrons relied on newspaper *articles* to find out about arts events, there was a drop from 48 percent to 36 percent over those three years. Similarly, the influence of *advertising* in newspapers dropped from 34 to 26 percent. That's a decrease of nearly 25 percent over a three-year period. To market researchers, that's a cataclysmic change.

How do you find out about arts events near your home?

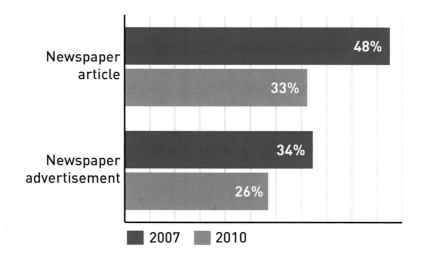

This research shows why newspaper executives have been sweating for the last couple of years: They see their influence falling dramatically, right in front of their eyes. The data are clear and consistent across several marketing sectors.

As you would expect, there's another media type stepping in to fill the void where newspapers once dominated. The Internet was the only mass-communications medium (a category in which we include television, radio, print newspaper, and magazines) that consumers told us they were using *more* over the three-year period from 2007 to 2010.

Every other media type experienced a drop in consumer use.

Arts patrons' media usage compared to previous year

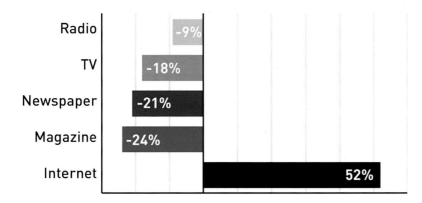

The consumer shift from analog to digital has been going on for the last decade, and these data codify exactly how dramatic it is. Your audience is moving steadily online, and if your marketing plans are not adjusting to this change, now is the time to recalibrate your efforts. There's scant evidence that this trend will reverse, and if anything, the introduction of better mobile Internet devices (such as the iPad) will likely increase the pace.

3. E-mail is the frontrunner to take print's place

Increasingly, patrons are adopting e-mail as their preferred means of receiving information about arts organizations. And it's not just any information that they value—they want to know what you are producing, and when. We asked respondents to rate the effectiveness of e-mail in terms of *keeping them updated about arts events in their community.*

Which of the following media types is most effective in keeping you updated about an arts organization?

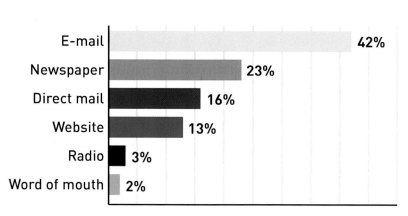

More than 40 percent of respondents in 2010 indicated that e-mail was the most effective medium of communication for them, a far greater percentage than any other media type.

When we asked how effective e-mail is for *knowing about last-minute offers*, its power became even more obvious: Nearly 80 percent indicated that e-mail is the most effective medium for this purpose; nothing else even comes close.

We don't advocate stopping marketing methods that still work—print mail can still have its place in your marketing plan—but you are working in a tricky environment, where different sectors of your audience prefer communicating via different types of media. When we asked survey respondents if they would like to receive e-mail or postal mail, nearly 50 percent said they *preferred* e-mail.

Which of the following best describes your preference for receiving arts marketing materials?

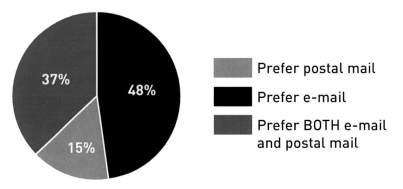

You should become ever more aware of the return on investment for both of these media types so that you can optimize your marketing spending. If you're sending out printed brochures to a lot of people who would prefer to hear from you via e-mail only, you're wasting money, and your response rates probably indicate that. There's no rocket science involved in finding out which people fall into which category. You simply have to ask them.

4. E-mail connects patrons to arts organizations

E-mail does more than just keep people informed. We asked our survey respondents to compare two arts organizations in their community: one that sends them regular e-mail newsletters and one that doesn't communicate with them via e-mail.

We saw some remarkable responses. About 78 percent said that regularly receiving e-mails makes them "better informed" about the organization, and 62 percent said they "feel more connected" to the organization whose list they were on. Similarly, 62 percent responded that they attend the organization's events more often when they're on the mailing list. (If that's not a compelling reason to get as many people signed up for your e-mail list as possible, we don't know what is.)

Gene relates personally to these survey results. He lives down the street from Jazz at Lincoln Center, and ever since the venue opened, he had wanted to attend. Yet when the time came to make plans, he would never think of it.

So Gene decided to sign up for their e-mail list, because he knew that their e-mails would be a regular reminder for him that he'd like to go. Every month, he gets one or two e-mails telling him what's going on.

The next time he had a friend visiting from out of town who said, "What's a cool thing I could do in New York?" Gene immediately remembered, "Jazz at Lincoln Center! Now's the moment to go see some jazz!" Because the club sent him monthly e-mails, it was on his mind.

Beyond ticket sales and attendance, e-mail is beginning to have an effect on the propensity of patrons to make donations to arts organizations. At this point it's a small influence, with only 16 percent indicating that they're more likely to make a charitable contribution because they receive e-mail, and 7 percent saying they'd be likely to give a larger amount because they received an e-mail. For fundraising purposes, the needle is moving a little bit in your favor if you send e-mail. It will likely continue to do so as people get more used to communicating with arts organizations over e-mail, and as you use the medium with greater sensitivity.

One of the questions arts marketers ask us most frequently is how often to send e-mail. So we asked your patrons: 86 percent said they wanted to hear from the organization at least once a month, and 33 percent preferred two or more times a month. If you already produce a monthly e-mail newsletter, you're probably in good shape. On the other hand, if you're not sending a newsletter at least once a month, you need to communicate with your patrons more regularly.

The survey did provide one data point that suggests some marketers are mailing too often. While 71 percent of patrons indicated that the arts e-mail newsletters they receive come with "just about the right frequency," 27 percent said that the newsletters come more frequently than they'd like. We interpret this to mean that e-mail newsletters have started to reach the saturation point. In Chapter 5, we'll discuss how to avoid overwhelming your patrons by sending targeted, relevant e-mail messages.

5. Online ticketing is now ubiquitous

What we found out about ticketing really shows how much the world has changed over the past few years. Online ticket purchasing is now mainstream. Thirty-five percent of respondents indicated that they had purchased tickets online in the past *week*, and 73 percent said they had used the Internet to buy tickets at least once in the past year. On average, 60 percent of arts patrons said they "most often" buy their tickets for cultural events online.

How do you most often buy tickets for arts events?

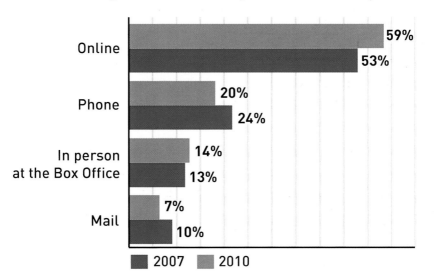

	2007	2010
Online	53%	59%
Phone	24%	20%
In person at the Box Office	13%	14%
Mail	10%	7%

Patrons have also said they would like to use the Internet to purchase and manage their subscriptions. Approximately 73 percent in 2009 expressed a desire to buy subscriptions online, up from 64 percent in 2006. However, today only a very small number of organizations offer online subscription purchasing—in 2010, only 36 percent of respondents said they had used the Internet to buy or renew a subscription in the past year.

This shift in ticket-buying preference is not limited to younger patrons. Online purchasing has the lead for the over-55 age group as well:

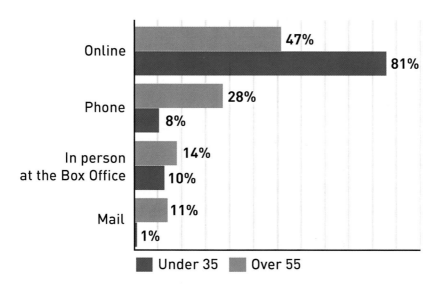

How do you most often buy tickets for arts events? (by age group)

E-commerce as a way of life for Americans has moved from a peripheral experience to one that is firmly embedded in everyday life. This is true across age ranges and product categories—today, Amazon.com, which started as an online bookstore in 1995, is an $80-billion company and competes with Walmart in selling appliances, electronics, and products of all kinds. What our survey data show is that consumers see online ticketing as an e-commerce experience just like any other, and that they *expect* to be able to transact online with every arts organization.

6. Some single-ticket buyers will never subscribe... but that's okay

The model of arts marketing that was codified back in 1977 in a book called *Subscribe Now*, by Danny Newman (in many circles still considered to be the bible for arts marketing), preached that your marketing efforts should focus on turning every single-ticket buyer into a subscriber. Newman viewed the long-term, repeatedly renewed subscription as the gold-standard relationship that your organization should aspire to develop with a patron. He viewed the single-ticket buyer as basically a noncommittal slug who ought not be afforded the same level of service or benefits as the revered subscriber.

In one sense, it's hard to find fault with Newman's approach. After all, you get a lot of money in advance from a subscription, which helps cash flow, and at the same time you minimize the unpredictability about what your overall ticket sales will look like. From the perspective of an arts organization, the benefits of the subscription model are clear.

But audience development ultimately should *not* be about your organization—it should be about your patron. Not all patrons are created equal, and not all patrons need or want subscriptions.

Perhaps Newman knew this as well, but his thinking was limited by the constraints of the era. In the 1970s, the investment in direct mail, print ads, and the like was high, and the only return on investment that made any sense was for a marketing effort pitched at a subscriber, where the average purchase price was high. While Newman was in favor of developing relationships, his worldview was colored by the economic realities of marketing at the time.

Today, in the age of CRM and social media, your marketing options are many, and the cost structures are lower. There are now plenty of ways of inexpensively connecting with patrons, even when they *aren't* subscribers and may never be.

Our data clearly show that there are a lot more single-ticket buyers than subscribers. Here's what our survey respondents report about their arts attendance:

Genre	Attended	Subscribed
Art museum	88%	40%
Theatre	77%	33%
Classical music	72%	29%
Dance	54%	15%
Opera	40%	15%

Note: The survey was not specific about what a "subscription" is, and we made no distinction among specific types, such as mini-subscriptions, make-your-own, or fixed subscriptions.

Relative to forty years ago, people have many more choices about how to spend their time. This may lead to a desire to be able to make more spontaneous decisions, with fewer patrons willing to make commitments far in advance. Our research supports our theory that those who subscribe may do so because a subscription satisfies a particular personality type more than because of any marketing efforts: 66 percent of people who said they subscribed to one genre actually said they subscribe to *multiple* genres.

These data indicate there are people who will always subscribe, simply because they are "subscribers." Subscriptions make them feel complete and organized. But there are a greater number of others who will *never* buy a subscription, not because they don't like your programs, but because their lifestyle simply doesn't work that way.

These non-subscribers still buy tickets, though:

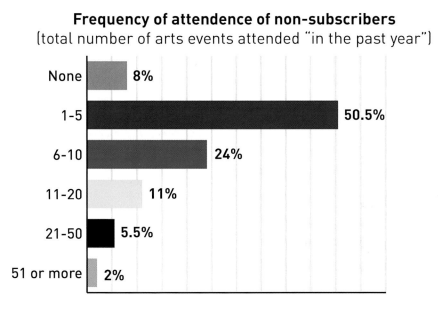

Frequency of attendance of non-subscribers
(total number of arts events attended "in the past year")

None	8%
1-5	50.5%
6-10	24%
11-20	11%
21-50	5.5%
51 or more	2%

Forty-three percent of non-subscribers attended more than five events per year! If you cultivate those single-ticket buyers and encourage repeat attendance, you may end up with the same financial result as you would get if they had subscribed. You might think of this as going after what credit-card marketers would call "share of wallet." If you know patrons are going to go to eight cultural events a year, then your job is to make sure that a higher and higher portion of those events are yours, whether or not they make an advance commitment. This is potentially your biggest opportunity to expand your audience.

Either way, to follow the *Subscribe Now* bible and treat single-ticket buyers differently from subscribers, exactly the approach many arts organizations still take, is to miss out on a huge audience-development opportunity.

As an industry, the arts seem overly obsessed with finding the "arts audience of the future." Every season, marketers commit tons of money toward new-audience development, because a relatively large percentage of last year's audience never comes back.

Finding new audiences then becomes a life-or-death situation for many organizations. And unfortunately, the guidelines of many grants programs traditionally invite managers to focus on initiatives that will get new patrons in the door, creating incentives for managers to overspend in this area. But by focusing so intently on new audiences, arts managers overlook the audience that's already attending their events. We believe that your "new audience" might already be sitting in your house!

Audience-development efforts need to recalibrate and move beyond the laser-beam focus of hunting down new patrons. Instead, what arts marketers should be doing is spending at least as much time and money nurturing existing audiences as they do finding new ones.

As an example, arts organizations offer benefits to their donors, such as CDs, tote bags, discounts on gift shops, and the like. Why not use these same tactics to reward your frequent attendees—simply because they come often?

7. Arts patrons seek a personal connection

What if we told you that the particular art you put on the stage isn't so important after all?

For some of your patrons, this may be true. Although the accepted wisdom is that what happens on the stage or hangs on the wall is the key driver of audience development, followed by price, there's now another factor that seems surprisingly crucial.

Fifty percent of the total audience surveyed said that if they "felt that an arts organization knew them personally," they would be *more likely to attend* that organization's events. What it says to us is that going to an arts event is not like going to a movie, where the film on screen is the attraction and your relationship with the theatre is only incidental. Arts attendance is intensely personal, and the data suggest that a large segment of your patrons wants the experience to be even more personalized.

Patrons today are now routinely experiencing "one-to-one" marketing from big retailers, their car-repair shops, or their local restaurant—they follow businesses on Twitter or Facebook and get personalized e-mails and direct-mail offers—and of course they are ready for their favorite arts organization to do the same.

If you know something about a patron—their preferences; their interests; their frequency of giving, attending, or even opening your e-mails—and you use that information to target messages to them that are highly personal, you're on your way. Too many organizations click the "send to all" button on their e-mail campaigns, mailing the same generic message to everyone, which is exactly the opposite of what connection-seekers are looking for.

The surprising thing about connection-seekers—that 50 percent whose attendance is influenced by "feeling connected"—is their lack of particular demographics. Though we tried, we could not find any demographic vector (age, income, gender) that significantly differentiated the connection-seekers from others. This means that there is layer across your entire audience that wants to be more connected, and you cannot simply use age or income segmentation to find them.

Back when he was running the American Symphony Orchestra, Gene could have used this kind of approach in a big way. At the core of the orchestra's mission, the music director would program music by composers that few patrons were familiar with. The marketing department then had to labor mightily to introduce this "unsellable" music to people through traditional means. Had the tools we'll discuss in the next few chapters been available then, they could have reached out to their audience in a much more personal way, and brought people into the hall based on the orchestra's relationship with them, and not based on simply the name of the composer.

Now, take a few moments to think about the trends, opportunities, and challenges facing the arts marketer today. If the first decade of the 21st century was a wake-up call to all marketers announcing that the world has changed, then the second decade will surely be one in which the best techniques, tools, and strategies will make winners out of organizations that choose to follow them. In the chapters to follow, we will dive into the specifics of building an effective e-mail program, improving your website, leveraging social media, and adopting CRM systems to build and communicate with a loyal patron base in the 21st century.

SECTION II: E-mail

Chapter 3

The Least Exciting but Most Effective Marketing Tool

Back in 2001, Gene's book *Wired for Culture* began:

> Fellow arts marketers, there's a new and fantastic world of e-mail marketing waiting at your fingertips…. I invite you to open your minds to the new world of e-mail marketing!

Ten years later, the vast majority of arts organizations has incorporated e-mail as a standard component of their overall marketing programs. However, despite this level of adoption, there's evidence that the arts field hasn't completely come around to understanding just how valuable e-mail marketing can be. There seems to be a stasis when it comes to e-mail.

Sixty percent of the patrons we surveyed in our national study said that overall, the quality of the arts e-mail newsletters they receive has "remained about the same" in the past year. Only 30 percent said they've gotten better. To us, this indicates that organizations are not investing enough creative or strategic energy into their e-mail communications.

Many only send out what they refer to as "e-blasts," one-shot mailings designed to fill empty seats. E-mail certainly can be an important factor in ticket sales, but e-mail can also be an incredibly effective way to share information with your audience, and make them feel connected to your organization.

For those who need a refresher as to why e-mail is such an effective tool for breaking the Fifth Wall, let's quickly review the six reasons e-mail is uniquely powerful.

1. E-mail is a form of *push* marketing. With e-mail, you are sending information out to your patrons when you want to, and when it makes sense for your organization, as part of your overall marketing program. E-mail allows you to actively break the Fifth Wall by reaching out to people instead of waiting for them to come to you.

Your website might be beautiful, flashy, and full of good information. But unlike with e-mail, your website can only reach people when *they* decide to visit. They may decide to come at a time disadvantageous for you, perhaps the day *after* your big event. And when they do come (if at all), you can't control what they look at, how much they pay attention, or how long they stay.

When someone joins your e-mail list, you have them in your orbit. You can then *push* an e-mail out to them at the time you determine is optimal. With e-mail, you own the relationship, because you control the marketing dialogue.

Since arts organizations are generally event-driven, it makes sense to dedicate significant resources to tools that can target your marketing effort to reach patrons around *your* event schedule.

2. E-mail is inexpensive. If you send a traditional direct-mail season brochure, you'll probably spend about a dollar on each one, and maybe half that for a printed postcard. With e-mail, you'll spend one-fiftieth of that price. When you do a return-on-investment (ROI) analysis and figure out exactly how much money you've brought in for how much invested, you may find that the direct-mail piece brings in the same amount of revenue as e-mail, but with e-mail your ROI is much higher.

Here's a chart that lays out a typical e-mail ROI scenario compared with direct mailing.

ROI Comparison - Campaign to 10,000 patrons (Average sale: two tickets at $45)

	Direct mail	E-mail
Cost to send	$5,000 ($0.50)	$200 ($0.02)
Response rate	1% - 100 buyers	26% open; 4% click-thru; 25% of those buy - 100 buyers
Revenue generated	$9,000	$9,000
Return on investment	$4,000	$8,800

3. E-mail is established. There are about 300 million people in the United States, and about 180 million people online over the age of 18.[3] Of those, 80 percent use e-mail.[4] Other means of communication online are less established and have far fewer users; for example, Twitter is a popular social media site, but it currently reaches only about 5 percent of the population.[5]

4. E-mail is green. In recent years, our society has warmed to the notion that it's good to do things that are energy efficient. E-mail doesn't generate paper unless people print it out, which makes it a lot more ecologically sound than mailing a brochure that costs many more trees and a lot more energy to produce, send, and deliver.

5. E-mail is preferred. When we asked in our survey of arts patrons how they like to receive information from arts organizations, 51 percent said they *prefer* receiving e-mail, while only 14 percent preferred postal mail. Clearly, e-mail has ascended. Again, we are not suggesting you drop your print promotions entirely, but be aware there's a healthy segment of your audience that has moved away from print, and you should adapt to that new reality.

6. E-mail casts a big shadow. There's a famous *New Yorker* cartoon that says it all: Two dogs are sitting in front of a computer screen. One dog looks at the other and says, "On the Internet, nobody knows you're a dog."

A well-designed e-mail from your small organization can look just as good as one from an organization with a budget ten times the size of yours.

When Gene was the Executive Director of the American Symphony Orchestra in New York City. One reason why it was such a challenging job was because they were a tiny orchestra with a $3 million budget, just five blocks away from the New York Philharmonic. He had board members who didn't understand (or didn't want to understand) the fact that they were not the New York Philharmonic.

The board members would say, "We have to be in *The New York Times*, that's where everybody looks." So Gene would take the small marketing budget he had for each of their Carnegie Hall concerts and buy minuscule ads in *The New York Times*. These were known as horizontal "strip ads," about one quarter of an inch high, appearing in the Sunday arts section.

But he knew that the *Times* never motivated very many ticket sales. The orchestra would have a presence in the paper, but was completely overshadowed by its competitors.

What Gene also knew was that the same amount of spending on radio advertising would in fact motivate ticket sales. The key difference between radio and newspaper advertising was that if they produced a high-quality thirty-second radio ad, it would sound just as good as the New York Philharmonic's ad. For those thirty seconds, the ASO and the NY Phil would be on a level playing field.

But one quarter of an inch in *The New York Times* next to an enormous half-page ad for the New York Philharmonic didn't look good no matter *what*! In the pay-by-the-inch land of print, they couldn't hide the fact that they were a tiny organization.

In the online world, e-mail is much like radio advertising. It can project a brand image to your patron that belies a meager budget.

7. E-mail is effective. Despite the strength of these seven axioms, e-mail marketing still suffers an identity crisis. It's not the most exciting-sounding new technology anymore, if it ever was. But the research says it best: 62 percent of online arts patrons say that they *attend an organization's events more often* when they're on the e-mail list.

We hope that this quick review has reinforced why e-mail is the most valuable marketing tool for the arts. It's inexpensive, patrons want it, and when they get it, they respond.

Once you do decide to make e-mail an essential part of your marketing strategy and give it the attention, resources, and importance it deserves, you need to effectively execute a campaign. In the next three chapters, we'll delve into the three essentials all organizations need to focus on to make e-mail reach its potential.

Chapter 4

Build Your List

This first rule may be the least exciting to talk about, but it's the most important: You must build your e-mail list, aggressively and continually. Period.

E-mail offers great benefits in terms of building and maintaining relationships with your patrons, but if your e-mail list is small or full of people who haven't explicitly signed up to be on it ("opted-in"), you simply won't get your message across. You can have a fantastic strategy and great content and graphics, but positive results from e-mail marketing grow directly as you build a high-quality opt-in list.

When marketers get serious about e-mail marketing, they usually focus their attention on the form of the e-mail itself. They pour hours into tweaking the content, subject lines, and pictures. But active list-building is even more important than the actual content of your e-mails. Marketers often act as if their lists will grow magically and automatically. That's not going to happen.

Gene once did a consulting session for a museum about its e-mail marketing. He started by looking over the e-mails they were sending out. The newsletters and promotions all looked great; in fact, everything they were doing was right.

But the marketing director was getting a little agitated. She wasn't happy with the results they were getting, so she really wanted to hear that they were using bad subject lines or unattractive background colors—anything to explain their lack of e-mail success. She finally blurted out, "You're telling us we're doing everything right! There must be *something* we're not doing right."

Gene responded, "How many people come through the front door of your museum every year?" She said, "120,000." He asked, "And how many e-mail addresses do you have on your mailing list?" The answer was 2,000.

She then went into all the reasons why it would be difficult to collect e-mail addresses at the door: union issues, precedence, politics, etc. But Gene continued, "You can't get big results with such small numbers. You should be mailing to at least 20,000 people. Wouldn't your department be much more important in the general realm of your organization if you had a bigger mailing list? The one thing I'm going to recommend is that you build your e-mail list."

Two years later, he returned to find that they had mounted an effective e-mail-address-collection process, and had built their list to 25,000 names. The marketing department had become the most powerful one in the organization, because everyone in the museum wanted to put something in the newsletter. Marketing was fending off the development department and the museum shop, because it had a huge asset: a big e-mail list.

With all this emphasis on building e-mail lists comes the obvious question: Why not simply buy, rent, or swap them? The reasons not to are many and compelling. As you'll read in Appendix B about the CAN-SPAM act, the rules governing list rentals are complex, and compliance can be onerous. More importantly, the response rates for purchased lists are typically awful, because even if you buy the most targeted lists possible, the recipients still haven't *opted in* to receive messages from you—they will perceive these unsolicited e-mails as spam. Most e-mail service vendors, including Patron Technology, will not allow you to upload a purchased list into their system at all, because the spam-complaint rate for purchased lists is very high, which can compromise your vendor's ability to get your e-mails delivered in the first place. So our rule of thumb is to forgo list purchases, rentals, and swaps entirely.

There is an alternative approach to expanding your e-mail reach that is nearly as easy, completely legal, and much more effective. This involves swapping space in your e-mail newsletters. You reserve *space* in your e-mail for a message or offer from another nearby arts organization, and they do the same for you in return. The patrons on both lists see this as a value-add—an organization they know and like is passing on information that's relevant to them that they may not have known about. It's a win/win approach.

The larger your list, the more leverage you have to swap space. You should base the terms of your swap on the sizes of your lists, so if your list is twice as large as your partner's list, then you'll get two messages in their newsletter for every one that you include on their behalf.

In terms of e-mail marketing success, there is no more important factor than having a large, opt-in e-mail list. We recommend you devote at least *50 percent* of the total time you allocate to all e-mail marketing activities to building your list. Think about it all the time, and make it a constant part of your job. E-mail list building takes commitment and work, but in the end there is no substitute for it.

Arts Patrons Want Arts E-mail: All You Have to Do Is Ask

Whenever we ask our clients what percentage of e-mail addresses they have from the people who are *already participating* in events at their organization, the number they usually give is between 20 and 30 percent. That's just not good enough. If someone comes to your organization's venue, whether it's for an exhibit, a concert, or a lecture, and they leave without your collecting some information from them, you've lost an opportunity to break the Fifth Wall and develop an ongoing relationship with that patron.

The good news is that arts patrons, when asked properly (and once assured that they're not going to get bombarded with e-mail messages), will give you their e-mail addresses willingly.

Our survey data show that patrons feel positively about signing up for arts e-mail lists.

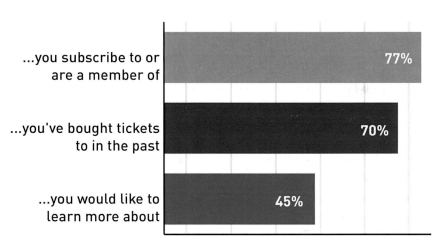

How likely would you be to sign up for the e-mail list of an arts organization...

...you subscribe to or are a member of — **77%**

...you've bought tickets to in the past — **70%**

...you would like to learn more about — **45%**

They are inviting you to market to them!

Patrons don't view arts organizations in the same way they view Procter & Gamble. You're not selling soap. People connect emotionally with what you do because arts organizations fuel their passions. Approach them with this in mind. Your appeal to get them to sign up should be, "We're so excited about our upcoming events and we want to share this information with you on a regular basis."

The Essentials of E-mail List Building

If your mission is to get as many of your patrons as possible to opt in for your e-mail list, you should integrate e-mail collection into every contact you have with your patrons. There's no "one thing" that's the secret to growing your e-mail list—the secret is doing ten or fifteen things right, and doing them continually.

The approach we advocate is that you utilize all the techniques you would use for any other type of institution-wide initiative you're used to mounting, such as the annual fundraiser or a subscription campaign.

With this in mind, here's a brief checklist of the kinds of things you'll need to put in place to mount an organization-wide e-mail list acquisition campaign.

1. **Buy-in at every level:** You're going to need the support of every level of your organization—from the board and executive director down to your part-time staff and volunteers. You must make the case that obtaining these e-mail addresses is as important to the mission of the organization as anything else you're doing.

Along the way, you're going to have to ask these people to step outside their traditional job roles to help you achieve your goal. Start by making sure you've sold them on the idea.

2. **Participation at every level:** As you'll see, many of the ideas that work best for growing your list may be done outside the traditional marketing or development department. You're going to need everyone—from your senior management to the box office staff, lobby staff, and the parking-garage attendant—to agree to take some of their time to help you. Everyone needs to understand they must play an active role here in helping to achieve your goal.

3. **Create incentives:** Nothing generates good feeling like rewarding your colleagues publicly for great work. You can reward individual efforts or entire departments.

The rewards need not be expensive. Dinner at a local restaurant or even a T-shirt is more valuable than you may think. There's an energy that's created as soon as you create a "bonus" structure, which will far outweigh the cost to you of the actual reward.

Announce your incentive plan to the staff, and include weekly or monthly goals. Have a plan to pick winners and a way to communicate who the winners are.

4. Create a time frame and goal: Your e-mail acquisition drive should have a start and end date, as well as a target number of e-mail names you'd like to collect.

5. Create a campaign plan: Just like a marketing plan for your organization, you'll need a formal plan describing exactly what you're going to do, who will do it, and when it will get done. The plan should also show expected outcomes. This need not be more than a page long.

6. Internal communications: Develop an internal progress report for your campaign. We've all seen the thermometer that measures success against a fundraising goal. These things really work!

7. Brand the plan and announce it to patrons and the public: Create a catchy name for your campaign, one that you can brand with consistent artwork.

Announce it to your patrons in every place you can. Use the same techniques you've used for years in fundraising campaigns. Once the goal is set and the time frame is announced, you've got a reason to keep people informed about what you're doing.

With this groundwork in place, let's move to the tactical side of your project. What exactly should you do?

Collection Techniques

Consider all the opportunities you have to connect with your patrons and get their e-mail addresses. If you've got a parking lot, why not put an e-mail sign-up card under every windshield? In your lobby, you have a wonderful opportunity to solicit your patrons. Don't put a box in the corner and then expect patrons to find it. Put together a roving band of volunteers with clipboards and t-shirts that say "Join Our List," who ask patrons to sign up. Once they're in the house, an insert in the program with a golf pencil taped to it will surely get patrons' attention.

At one Off-Broadway theatre in New York, the house manager comes on stage before each performance to welcome the audience, thank the corporate sponsors, and invite the audience to sign up for their e-mail list by filling out a card tucked into the program. Intermission presents another wonderful opportunity. Why not offer a free soft drink in exchange for every new e-mail address?

After the performance, volunteers can hand out e-mail sign-up forms as patrons exit, which they can exchange for a discount on parking when they leave the garage. If you're in an urban location where most people take public transportation, how about stationing volunteers there? We've never seen volunteers in the 66th Street subway station at Lincoln Center after a performance, but it would probably be so startling and unusual that it would work!

These are just a few ideas of things you can do at your venue. Needless to say, collecting e-mail addresses as part of a ticket purchase, subscription purchase, and donation solicitation are things you ought to be doing as a matter of course. Appendix C details many more obvious—and some less-than-obvious—ideas on building e-mail lists.

Chapter 5

Be Interesting

The second rule, "be interesting," lies at the heart of breaking the Fifth Wall with e-mail. In general, your marketing goal should be to engage with your patrons by feeding them an irresistible diet of information designed to ignite their passion and motivate them to return.

Remember the data we presented in Chapter 2: Patrons are reading arts e-mails less frequently and thoroughly than they used to. That means you've got to stand out from the masses and get people's attention.

Our catchphrase, "be interesting," encourages you to keep this in mind on all levels, from the content of your e-mails to the targeted groups you send to and how you entice people to open and read your mail. Let's examine each in turn.

Be Creative with Your Content

If you're really committed to building a relationship with your patrons, you've got to send them engaging, relevant, and timely information that will grab their attention and bring them closer to your organization. You're going to need to think beyond the common practice of sending "e-mail blasts" that go out at the last minute to drive ticket sales. To break the Fifth Wall, you need to reach beyond discounts and calendars.

Yes, your patrons want to know what events are happening at your organization, and your newsletters ought to include that information. But simply sending out a calendar listing is, frankly, boring. Of course, people respond to discount offers and promotions, and e-mail does a great job of announcing them, but those should not be the bulk of your e-mail content either.

Think about all of the interesting things going on in your organization that you never had space to feature when you published your newsletter in print. If you think hard enough you'll realize that you've got a wealth of interesting information to share.

While promoting your events, why not include behind-the-scenes photos or anecdotes, like, "Here's at a look at the progress of an installation on the roof of our gallery"? One art gallery does a series of articles teaching people how to collect art, called Collecting 101. Obviously, it's self-interested (the newsletter ends by saying, "Once you have educated yourself and have fallen in love with a work of art, buy it, take it home, and enjoy it!"), but it's something more than straight news about what's going on at the gallery this week.

Another museum has a monthly newsletter feature where it shares archival photographs that the public has never seen. A dance company featured a "ballet term of the month."

To start you off brainstorming about how to create great e-mail content, think about these three main categories of information about your organization, which you can use to generate content ideas: *people, products/productions,* and *place.*

Category A is the idea of writing about the **people who are involved with the organization**.

Your organization's **staff, artists, donors, volunteers, patrons, educators,** and **students** have a unique perspective and a distinct relationship with the organization. They are also your biggest advocates, and are likely to be passionate about the art or work produced. Your newsletter is a place where you can highlight their insights or opinions about the organization. In turn, you might ignite a new patron's passion for your organization

Category B refers to what your organization **produces**.

In most cases, your product is the particular **form of art presented** at your organization, in addition to the related programming that enhances the cultural experience. Rather than simply announcing new works and listing their dates, elaborate on your programs in the newsletter.

Think about the work that goes into creating the play on your stage or the sculpture in your gallery. Many of your patrons may want to have a behind-the-scenes taste of what it takes to produce your events.

Category C, *place*, refers to writing about the institution itself: its history, its traditions, and the physical space.

Chances are the people who run your organization have changed over time, but the institution has survived them. If you have moved locations, had multiple executive directors, built a new wing in your museum, or added a new hall to your venue, sharing a historical tidbit gives your patrons unique insight into your organization.

Another approach to e-mail content is to step outside the bounds of your organization and write about things that are currently on people's minds. For this we can offer an example very close to home. As you might imagine, at Patron Technology, we have a monthly e-mail newsletter with about 7,000 recipients, most of whom are arts managers and executives. Our editorial strategy has always been to offer articles about e-marketing to educate the field.

About a year ago, we looked at the statistics for our own e-mail newsletter, and we were pretty ashamed. We had a 15-percent open rate and a 1.3-percent click rate, much lower than the industry average. This was depressing—we're in the e-mail business! What could we do to get those numbers up?

Gene challenged the staff: "Our content is obviously boring our audience. We've got to revitalize what we do." So we brainstormed, and the next month we switched our focus from the "E-marketer of the Month" client interviews we'd been doing for years and instead started writing about more of-the-moment topics: Facebook, the economy, Twitter, fundraising...

When we did this, our open rate shot up to 19.9 percent, a 27-percent increase, and the click rate increased by over 300 percent to 5.4 percent.

All we did was write about different things! We didn't have a bigger list. We didn't use better technology. The change wasn't due to anything other than being relevant and interesting. Those are big-number results based on a very slight change on our part—one that cost us nothing but a few hours of thinking.

What we came away with from this example is the rule we're suggesting for you: Relevant content wins! Content is what will grab people's attention.

Making your content interesting can also be as simple as changing your tone. A great example of an e-mail that shows a lot of personality comes from the Brookfield Zoo in Chicago. Their newsletter is written for kids and is called "Animail," written by "Zookeeper Kris."

In one giraffe-themed issue of the newsletter, Kris opens with, "I'm not sticking my neck out when I tell you I have a TALL tale to tell this week." When parents receive the newsletter, we're guessing they share it on the computer, or print it out and read it to their children. We think this is a brilliant strategy, and their open rates prove it.

How boring it would have been to send a newsletter addressed only to parents, saying, "We've adjusted the zoo hours. We now have better parking..." That's an easy trap to fall into.

Great content is clearly a challenge, but publishing a boring newsletter is really not an option anymore for organizations that want their e-mails read. As we noted above, patrons are becoming more and more discriminating in terms of what they will open and read. As arts marketers, you'll have better success when you send a newsletter that stands out.

Write Effective Subject Lines

If you take away only one thing from this chapter, it should be this: The one part of your e-mail message that 100 percent of your recipients see is your subject line. Even if they don't open the e-mail, even if they delete it, the subject line still passes in front of their eyes. For that reason, you ought to treat your subject line as a highly valuable marketing message.

The subject line is a crucial component of your marketing because it's where you can combine your content message (what the e-mail is about) with your targeting (why it's relevant to the reader). The subject line must be recognizably relevant to the audience segment you're trying to reach.

In terms of subject-line content, our recommendation is to be clear, concise, and actionable. Tell your recipients what your e-mail is about, and be direct. Don't just write "teaser" text. Remember that for some portion of your recipients, the subject line is *all* they see. Simple and clear beats cute and clever every time.

Cute: "Spring Arts Fiesta Fun Time!"
Clear: "Spring Arts Festival Begins May 12"

Another tip to keep in mind: Subject lines should be short. Depending on the e-mail system your recipient is using, you have about 50 characters before the message will be cut off or will scroll to the next line. If you're in doubt about how your subject line will look in the inbox, it's pretty simple to test it. Just send an e-mail to yourself and others who use a different e-mail system from yours, and check how it displays.

Patron Technology	1:22 PM
E-mail Marketing Seminars for Arts Executives, Octobe...	

Patron Technology	1:17 PM
E-mail Marketing Seminars for Arts Execs, Oct 18-26	

If the format of your e-mail newsletter is consistent, your subject lines should be consistent too. Your regularly scheduled monthly newsletter should be instantly recognizable in your recipients' inboxes, so use a similar subject line each time. For instance:

"Lab Theatre News: Meet Our New Artistic Director" (one month)
"Lab Theatre News: Announcing the 2011-2012 Season" (the next month)

It's worth repeating: Since 70 to 80 percent of recipients for any individual e-mail campaign will read *only* your subject line, you should devote sufficient time and attention toward ensuring your subject lines are the most effective they can be.

It's easy to do some simple testing to find out what subject lines work the best for your audience. Next time you send out any e-mail campaign, take a few extra minutes to split your recipient list in half. Make sure that each half of your list has at least 1,000 names. This is what's commonly known as an "A/B test." Write two different subject lines for the same campaign, and send one to each list. See which version gets a higher open rate and click rate. Over time, you'll learn what kinds of subject lines your patrons respond to.

Target Your Audience

Part of being interesting is having great content, but the other part is getting the right content *to the right people*. Targeting your e-mails is important because the closer you match your patrons' interests with a message that's relevant to them, the more likely it is that they'll pay attention to it and do something about it.

If this sounds familiar, and similar to what you know about direct-mail marketing, you're right. E-mail is simply another form of direct marketing, in digital format. The more you embrace the rules of direct marketing, particularly the concept of targeting, the higher your response rates will be.

Some argue that since e-mail is so much less expensive than direct mail, marketers don't need to feel constrained by the rules of direct marketing. Why not simply e-mail everything to everyone? While the financial argument is compelling, *relevance* is what keeps people opening and reading your e-mail. Your recipients will eventually tune out irrelevant messages, and once this happens, it is very difficult to re-engage them. A mass-marketing approach to e-mail is the enemy of relevance.

The good news is that unlike in the direct-mail world, targeting can be simple and inexpensive. In our PatronMail system and most other e-mail systems, you can first enable patrons to identify their interests by placing themselves into *preference categories* when they sign up for your mailing list, and then target your mailings based on those categories. Do they want information about events for kids or teenagers, for example? Or if you're a touring company, you can have them indicate in which cities they want to attend performances.

Beyond the preferences your patrons indicate themselves, you probably also know some other things about the patrons on your e-mail list, and you can use that information to categorize them and send e-mails that are very specific to these categories. For instance, you can segment your list based on whether they are donors, how much and how frequently they donate, or whether they are students, subscribers, or first-time single-ticket buyers.

Behavioral Targeting

Even without categories based on patron interests or demographics, your e-mail system probably offers you a lot of data to work with.

When you send out e-mail, you should pay attention to your **open rate**, which represents the percentage of people who receive an e-mail and view it. (The average open rate for all PatronMail clients over a six-month period is around 20 percent.) Some recipients click on links within the e-mail; that's known as the **click rate**. (The average click rate for all PatronMail clients over a six-month period is around 2.35 percent.)

Any professional e-mail system will collect this information on an ongoing basis. Over time, your recipients will create a behavioral profile of themselves for you. Armed with this data, you can segment your e-mail lists into relevant marketing categories and send e-mail to people who will be interested to receive it. Depending on the kind of e-mail system you're using, this may be as simple as a few clicks, or it may involve exporting and importing lists to make this happen.

You'll likely find that there are three kinds of people on your e-mail list: the people who *always* open your e-mails, those who *sometimes* open, and those who *never* open. In the messages you send to those who open your e-mails all the time, you can easily create an ongoing editorial dialogue by referring back to content from previous months and really engaging your readers. You can write a series of articles that link together from month to month.

For those patrons who read only occasionally, you might want to have content that is episodic, or topical articles, such as an interview of the month, whose format allows the occasional reader to jump right in and immediately understand your subject.

For patrons who read nothing, the subject line will be your best chance to lure them inside. If you have a group of perpetual non-openers, you might survey them to try to identify what kinds of content they would like to see in an e-mail or newsletter. We've found that there's nothing like a survey to get people to respond!

If you're short on time and can't compose three different e-mails, try using the same content for all three but with different headers or lead-in sections.

Subject: Latest news from Lab Theatre

Dear So and So,
We know you're a **loyal patron**, and we wanted you to have the inside scoop....

LABORATORY THEATRE

Subject: Catch up with Lab Theatre

Dear Such and Such,
If it's **been a while** since you've heard what we're up to, we wanted to give you a chance to catch up!...

L**A**BORATORY THEATRE

Behavioral targeting can be a potent tool for the development department. A development director who can send an e-mail to the people who have opened each of the last six e-mails knows ahead of time that this is a responsive group of patrons. With this knowledge in hand, she could invite those particular patrons to a special event, or make a unique appeal.

The corporate world is obsessed with this kind of targeted marketing because it works. At a marketing conference a few years ago, the head of digital marketing for American Airlines described how five marketing managers do nothing but pore through this kind of data and write targeted e-mails for each segment. One example he gave was, "These are the people who live on the east coast who've gone to San Juan once in the last three years. We're going to send them a Caribbean discount offer." When you mine your data to that level, you always get better results than if you click "send to all."

We often hear people say, "Oh, but my list is too small for all this targeting stuff." First of all, you're never too small to target. If you're only e-mailing a limited number of people, the last thing you can afford to do is turn anyone off by sending an irrelevant message. And if your list is truly small, go back to the fundamental lessons about building your list.

Chapter 6

Be Professional

It's not enough to say, "I have a big e-mail list, and I'm 'doing e-mail marketing,' I can move on."

Rule three is that you need to be more professional, and take e-mail marketing as seriously as you take the preparation of your print materials. We have clients who have really great open and click rates all the time, and when we ask them how they do it, the answer is always the same: They focus on timing, design, and appearance.

Timing

To think professionally, you need to employ all your editorial techniques. The most obvious technique is to develop an annual editorial calendar with planned publishing dates. We have an e-mail newsletter calendar that covers the next six months. We know exactly when e-mails will go out; we know how long in advance we have to prepare them; we know if we're behind or ahead of schedule. If you wake up on Tuesday morning and say, "Uh-oh, we've got a show this weekend. I'd better rush off an e-mail!" you're not going to be as effective as you could and should be.

Design

E-mail design is different from print design, particularly when it comes to images. Images can be very effective in an e-mail, but you need to think carefully about how you use them. Image blockers exist in a lot of e-mail inboxes, and ever more people read their e-mail on mobile devices that only show text. Let's look at what can happen if you don't plan for this.

On the right is an e-mail mock-up for a fictitious dance group called the Bombastic Biddies. They sent out a newsletter to their mailing list of 2,000 names inviting people to an event on June 26th.

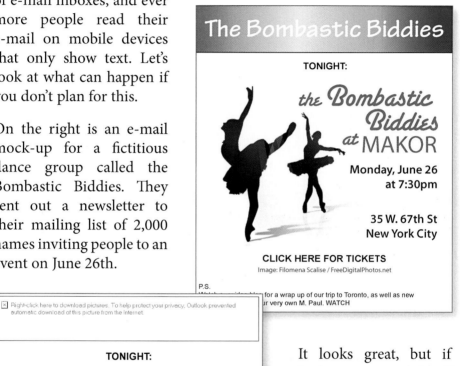

The Bombastic Biddies

TONIGHT:

the *Bombastic Biddies* at MAKOR

Monday, June 26
at 7:30pm

35 W. 67th St
New York City

CLICK HERE FOR TICKETS
Image: Filomena Scalise / FreeDigitalPhotos.net

P.S.
...for a wrap up of our trip to Toronto, as well as new ...ur very own M. Paul. WATCH

☒ Right-click here to download pictures. To help protect your privacy, Outlook prevented automatic download of this picture from the Internet.

TONIGHT:

☒ Right-click here to download pictures. To help protect your privacy, Outlook prevented automatic download of this picture from the Internet.

CLICK HERE FOR TICKETS
Image: Filomena Scalise / FreeDigitalPhotos.net

P.S.
Watch our video blog for a wrap up of our trip to Toronto, as well as new choreography from our very own M. Paul. WATCH

It looks great, but if images are turned off on your computer or on a mobile device, what you get is more like the picture to the left.

The important data are all locked up in the image, which includes the time, place, and date of the event.

Very often our clients work with an ad agency or designer to create a poster, and they think it's a good idea simply to send an image of the poster as an e-mail. But remember, what works in print is not necessarily what works in a digital medium. The translation can be tricky, and a flawed execution can backfire. Again, the people who have turned off images, or whose smartphone won't render images, won't see anything at all.

There is a simple solution for this. Go ahead and upload your image, but beneath it, repeat in text the most important information, because text is read by every e-mail system.

When we redid this newsletter, we created the campaign on the left. It looks pretty similar. The only difference is that we *repeated in text* the most important information so that folks who received a text-only version saw the e-mail on the right.

If this simple design change can pick up 10-percent more people who otherwise wouldn't have gotten your message, that's a big deal.

The real key to great e-mail design is to do everything you can to make sure your patrons see the information you want them to see. Besides being careful with graphics, you should also be aware that not all e-mail real estate is created equal. You want to be aware of what content appears "above the fold."

In this respect, e-mail design actually is a lot like designing for print. Think about people reading a printed newspaper. More people read the top of the front page than any of the interior pages. After the front page, they skim through the rest, perhaps reading in some depth only the front of each section.

E-mail has an equivalent to the front page. Those of you who use Microsoft Outlook know about the preview pane. That's the top part of the e-mail that you see on your screen before you even click "open" to read the whole e-mail.

In our research study we asked patrons who said they use a preview pane, "How much of the e-mail do you actually read when you get an e-mail newsletter?"

Only 24 percent said they read the entire e-mail. Don't assume people will scroll; 13 percent said they read just what's in the preview pane. Most important, 61 percent said, "I read just the first few lines." What this means is that 74 percent of the respondents did not look past the beginning of the e-mail.

On the next page, we've reprinted a sample of a typical arts newsletter with half a dozen articles. On the left is the preview pane view that shows what 74 percent of people saw when they received it.

As you can see in this example, it's quite easy to get around the "above the fold" problem. If you have a long newsletter with many articles, include an index or a list of headlines at the top of the e-mail, where each clickable headline sends the reader to the article below. In an indexed newsletter, everyone can see the entire contents in a glance, right there in the preview pane, and jump down to what's important to them. These article headlines act like mini subject lines, conveying a marketing message even if the article itself isn't read.

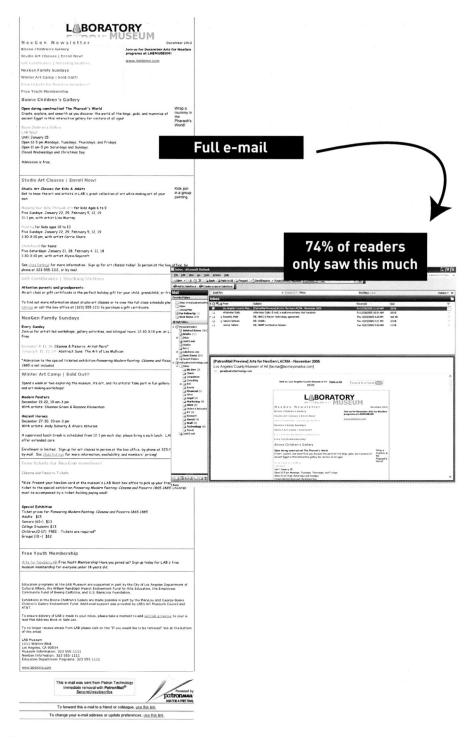

Here's another example of the kind of effect the "fold" can have on e-mail results. This is a newsletter from the **Edward Gorey House**.

The part that shows up in the preview pane is, of course, that first article.

You can see that as people had to scroll down to the bottom, the click rates declined. The data makes it clear: As you go farther below the fold, you're going to lose people's attention.

Keep this in mind when deciding on the order of content in your e-mail newsletters.

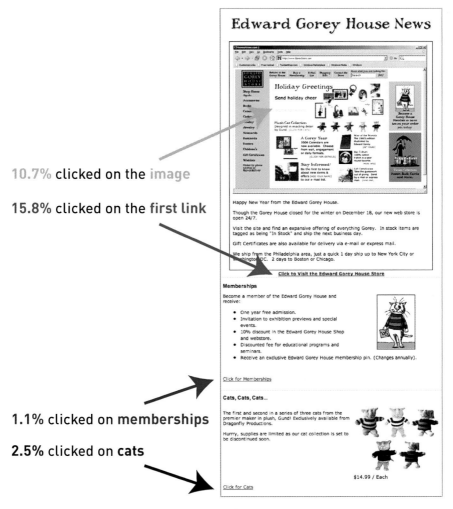

10.7% clicked on the image

15.8% clicked on the first link

1.1% clicked on memberships

2.5% clicked on cats

Proofread

We cannot emphasize enough the need to proofread everything that you send out. This may sound embarrassingly obvious, but every single week we get an urgent e-mail or phone call from a client who asks, "Could you please un-send that e-mail I just sent out?"

You must proofread.

The Laboratory Theatre is fictional, and we've exaggerated this example, but errors like the ones you see below are all too common in real e-mails we've received. At Patron Technology, we spend about $25 per e-mail campaign to hire a professional proofreader who gets the e-mail on Thursday night and returns it to us with changes on Friday morning. That $25 buys us a lot of security. What is that peace of mind worth in terms of the brand and image of your organization? Would you send off a print brochure without first proofing it three or four times?

If you can't afford a professional proofreader, one of your subscribers would probably do the work for free. Even if you just give an e-mail to somebody in the office who didn't work on it and has never seen it before, you'll get a better result than simply rereading it yourself. And there may be no scientific reason for this, but simply sending a preview of an e-mail to yourself and others on staff (before sending it to patrons) has a way of teasing the eyes to pick up errors.

However you do it, you need to proofread, even several times.

These three essentials of e-mail marketing—build your list, be interesting, be professional—are by no means the only things about e-mail that need concern you. But if you get these three things right, you'll be executing professional e-mail campaigns and avoiding the most common pitfalls.

We want to end with a final point that's often misunderstood, but which ultimately reconnects to our theme about how e-mail helps you break the Fifth Wall.

Think about your open rates. The average open rate for our e-mail clients is only about 20 percent. But that's a somewhat misleading statistic, because it only represents a single e-mail campaign in time.

A more interesting measure is to look at the average *cumulative* open rate—how a fixed group of patrons on a mailing list responds over time. We have found that about two thirds of them will open at least *one* e-mail from an organization over a six-month period.

That two thirds is made up of some people who open all the time, some who open occasionally, and some who may open only once in a six-month time frame. Thus, if you are getting a consistent 25-percent open rate, that doesn't mean you're reaching only 25 percent of your audience. The makeup of that 25 percent is not the same from month to month. The "other 75 percent" of people on your e-mail list aren't simply all a big group of slackers!

The point is, if you send e-mail newsletters consistently, using enticing subject lines and mailing to targeted lists, you'll eventually break the Fifth Wall for a lot more than 25 percent of the people on your list.

E-mail marketing has come a long way in a few short years. It may not be the newest and most exciting tool, but we urge you to do it well. Of all the other technologies we discuss in this book, e-mail is the most powerful and cost-effective marketing tool there is.

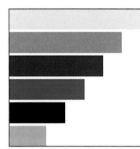

SECTION III:
Websites, Ticketing, and the User Experience

Chapter 7

Six Principles for Great Arts Websites

We have placed this chapter about arts websites after our discussion of e-mail marketing to make a point. In the imaginary movie called "online arts marketing," websites are the supporting actor, not the star. That's because unlike e-mail, which is an active or "push" marketing technique, websites are entirely passive. They only work if your patrons visit them! And they only work if your patrons look at the pages you want them to look at. Both of these factors are entirely controlled by the site visitor, not by you, the marketer.

That said, arts websites do play an important role in breaking the Fifth Wall, by receiving visitors who come looking for information. Your site's visitors arrive from a variety of sources: e-mail marketing, Google searches, event listings, links from other websites, etc. Just like your e-mail marketing, your website ought to offer incredibly compelling content and a design that will draw these visitors in, engage them with your mission and your artistic product, and continue to connect their passions with your organization.

Before you begin reading this chapter, you may not think your website needs revamping. But we suspect that once you get through it, you'll realize there are improvements to be made. We're not necessarily suggesting you throw out what you have and start over, but you may decide that investing some time and money into sprucing things up is necessary.

The problem of most arts websites is that many of the most crucial design decisions are based on gut instinct and personal preference.

To design an effective website, consumer brands regularly spend millions on professional research to assess their sites. Without such research, website quality is hard to judge, because there are no commonly accepted benchmarks that can help you understand if your arts website is good or not.

You may be tracking your site usage statistics using Google Analytics (which we highly recommend), but these data don't really tell you very much about how your patrons *like* your site, nor do they offer much insight on how to design it.

To address this lack of benchmarks, we conducted our own research. We looked closely at a range of arts websites in order to derive our own concepts and standards against which to assess their effectiveness.

Because there's such wide variety among arts websites, we decided against a broad statistical survey. Instead, we conducted focus-group studies specifically about arts websites, to get at the essence of what arts patrons really think about them, and what they want from them.

Two groups of arts patrons came together in a professional focus-group facility in the summer of 2009 in St. Louis. We showed them three-dozen arts websites and solicited written and oral reactions from them. The entire project was managed and analyzed by the professional market research firm BlueBear LLC, which specializes in website quality assessment focus groups for Fortune 500 companies.

Surprisingly, we found consistent results across the sites we looked at. The biggest news we have is that the overall website assessments by our panelists did not correlate with the budget size of the organizations they were looking at. This is good news for small organizations because, just like with e-mail, it means they can present themselves just as well online as large organizations. Some of the smallest organizations with modest resources had just as strong results as organizations with ten times the budget size. This means you can't get away with the excuse, "We don't have a big enough budget to have a great website!"

A second major discovery was that we found very little difference in patrons' reactions across arts genres. We researched a wide variety of organizations, from theatres and orchestras to dance companies, university presenters, and museums. We're now confident in saying that the success of an arts website has nothing to do with genre, either.

Here's a final piece of news; though somewhat obvious, it may send shivers up your spine: Patrons told us that if an arts organization has a poor website, it suggested to them that what they would eventually see on stage would also be poor. That has massive implications, since your website is often the first (and maybe only) interaction your patrons will have with your organization before they attend an event. If your website doesn't present a good first impression, your "performance" has already gotten a bad review.

From this experience of talking directly with patrons, we were able to identify consistent reactions that can guide the design and development of all arts sites. These should help you assess the quality of your own organization's site and assist you in making improvements to it. We've boiled down these findings into six basic principles for great arts websites:

1. Put the basic information up front.

It is amazing how many arts organizations don't put their most basic information in an obvious place on their website. No matter how much educational content you have on your site, or how much descriptive information you offer about your art, the fact is that the main reason people go to an arts site is to find out *what's* happening, *where* it's happening, and *when* it's happening.

They need location, directions, address, time: all the basics. Yet often these details are buried as if they belonged in the appendix of a book.

When you design your site, put yourself in the place of someone coming to the website for the very first time. What does a first-time visitor need to know about this organization? Go back to your site and see how hard it is to find basic information. Count the mouse clicks. If they go beyond two, start redesigning.

Make sure your main page includes a phone number and a link to the box office, as well as a way to donate. Include mundane things as well: information about parking, food service, maps, public-transportation schedules and the like.

We all know how important the mission of the organization is, but frankly, people's basic questions need to be addressed first, like "How do I get there?" and "How do I get home?"

2. Capture the experience and stir the emotions.

Your site should give a patron the feeling or flavor of what the experience will be like at the performance itself. One of our respondents said, "Give me the feeling like I'm there."

You can best do this through photography or design, not words. Websites that merely *talk* about "uplifting experience" will never be able to *convey* that feeling. You need to offer a visceral experience created with images, a slide show, or even video.

Another respondent commented on a site she liked: "[In] the few pictures that were there, the performers made me feel like I was there too."

The image from the **American Shakespeare Center** below shows an example of a site that successfully pulls the viewer into the experience.

As you can see, the vivid photography captures the faces of the performers, shows exactly what to expect, and draws in the viewer.

Not only do you need to capture the experience, but you need to stir the emotions. A big, dramatic photo with a sense of motion can help achieve this.

Of course, you can't put up just any image. We got tremendous numbers of positive comments on photography that showed *people in action*. It's one thing to show a symphony orchestra in a posed shot. It's quite another to focus on the dramatic sweep of a conductor's baton with the violins digging in at a climactic moment. We showed patrons a website for a symphony orchestra that had no pictures of musicians on it, just an image of two tulips. One patron said, "Tulips have nothing to do with an orchestra." The tulips were nice, but what relationship did they have to the art on the stage? Disconnected images like these are exactly what you don't want. But an active, engaging, and emotionally charged image will get people involved from their heart.

It's worth mentioning that years ago, the rule of thumb on the web was to keep all photos small. That made sense when most of the population was connecting online using a slow dial-up service. However, as fast Internet connections are now the norm, image size is no longer a key consideration for your website.

The implication here is that photography may be the single largest expense of your website. But it's worth it, because it will capture the essence of who you are. As we know from extensive data, your site visitors spend very little time on your site. They are likely reading much less than you would like them to. But images make an instant impression. If you show them a compelling photo, your patrons will get it, and you won't need to worry endlessly about just the right copy.

3. Stake a unique claim.

Let's recall Brand Development 101: Your organization needs to have a clearly distinguishable brand, and you must communicate that brand on your website in a way that tells your patrons how your organization stands out from all others. Remember, your patrons are looking at your competitors' sites as well.

This means you've got to come up with a single clear idea that differentiates your organization's site to visitors, and does so instantly. Patrons must be able to think, "Wow, this organization is special and unique because of X or Y." If your site is generic or neutral, you will have much less of an impact on your visitors.

The **Pilobolus Dance Company** offers a great example of a unique site. Take a look at their main screen below.

The site features strikingly unique photography, which makes a distinct claim: This is dance unlike all other. It's fresh, new, and exciting. With very little text, the site still makes the point about why this company is different and worth seeing.

One respondent said of this site, "Cool, provocative, absolutely perfect, not everyone's dance company." Notice how he mixed up the website with the dance company itself. That's exactly the effect you should be going for.

When you stake a bold aesthetic claim, you will lose some people, but you'll pick up others with even more fervor. This is true with any product in any category: The more intense your brand image, the more intense the relationship with your client base can be. Just look at the intensity with which people love—or hate—Apple computers or Starbucks. The most important thing is to make sure that you know what you stand for and that your website communicates your message to the patron. They need to know it too.

4. What's playing now?

Be timely. Make sure your site shows what's happening right now. You need to offer the user a sense of urgency and vitality. There's nothing more unfortunate than a site that has outdated events on the main screen.

We constantly see websites with last month's schedule. Some even have last *season's* schedule! If you don't show viewers what's coming up, they will take away the message that no one from your organization is paying any attention to its own work.

5. Keep it simple.

Simplicity is probably the hardest thing to maintain as a design principle when developing a website, since websites are inherently complex.

But the most frequent negative comments we got from our panelists were about website complexity. People looked at site after site and said things like, "too much going on, don't know what to read first," when faced with websites that were filled with too much information. One respondent commented that the home page of a site looked "like a TV-channel lineup."

If you are clear and lay out your information in a simple and easy format, people will appreciate it. A powerful photograph, simple navigation with clear links, and a logical hierarchy are all you really need. As the saying goes, when in doubt, keep it simple.

6. Design matters.

The design choices you make must be strategic decisions that reflect your brand. Design brings the parts together as a whole, combining tone, color, images, language, and graphics.

Look at the website below for **Theatre by the Lake**, in the U.K. The elements that matter are the surreal photography, the muted colors, and the simple design. There's nothing extraneous here.

Take a moment to visit your website with these six principles in mind. Be tough on yourself about how you're doing with each one. Remember that your website is your organization's public face, and in only a few seconds it can make or break a new relationship with a patron.

By now we hope you've opened yourself to the idea that your site—anyone's site—needs some improvement. Thus far, we've focused on the consumer experience of your website. This is a crucial perspective and vital for breaking the Fifth Wall. But it's not everything.

No matter how well your site is designed and no matter how much it aligns with our six design principles, it won't really be effective unless you have a coherent *strategy* in place. The next chapter assumes that your site is already designed well, and within that framework offers guidance on how to ensure that it meets your marketing objectives.

Chapter 8

Your Website Is a Marketing Tool

As we just explained, most arts websites could be better. But this doesn't only mean their design could be better or their technology could be more cutting-edge. Rather, the frustrating thing about most of the sites we've viewed is that they clearly don't support the marketing and fundraising goals of their organizations. Most are loosely organized, rambling, and ultimately ineffective.

The root of this ongoing problem probably lies in the early years of the web, when arts marketers quickly built websites that were nothing more than season brochures in digital form. Designed to offer a salad bar of information, most were casually organized and based on the idea that visitors would take the time to poke around and find the information they were seeking.

The web has matured, and we now know that websites shouldn't just be an exhaustive collection of pages about an institution. Rather, they need to be organized strategically, just like any other marketing tool.

Websites as "Machines For Engagement"

So, how do you produce a great arts website? Let's start with a definition:

A *great arts website* is a carefully structured collection of web pages designed and organized to achieve a measurable goal, one that supports your organization's overall mission as well as your bottom line. A great arts website offers visitors the information they want in the fastest way, with the fewest number of mouse clicks and the least amount of confusion.

This ideal kind of website is *conceptually* a "machine for engagement." Just like a physical machine that has input and output, the input on a website is your patrons' time and attention, and the output is information that motivates them to think differently, participate in your programs, and interact with your organization in some way.

We encourage you to begin with this question:

What did the people who visited my site today come away with?

Understand the Needs of Your Web Audience

Your website won't help you break the Fifth Wall until you understand your site's visitors. How much do you truly know about their needs?

Here are some basic questions to have in mind:

- What do visitors expect when they come to your site?

- What do they think they want to accomplish on your site? (e.g., register for a class, buy a ticket, make a donation)

- What kind of information are they seeking?

- How do visitors know about your site? What impressions and assumptions do they bring with them? Are you supporting an existing image or creating a new one?

- What portion of your visitors are current ticket buyers, members, or fans? New visitors whose first impression of your organization will come from your site?

- What is their impression of your site after viewing it for the first time?

- For regular visitors, what information have they returned to obtain? How frequently do they visit your site?

- Are there places on your site where visitors can easily make a purchase or transaction, ask a question, or send an inquiry?

If you don't have a clear answer for each of these questions, you can't build a site that effectively meets your needs. There's no magic in discovering the answers. All you need to do is ask, by doing your own research. Though we spent thousands of dollars doing sophisticated marketing research in a professional focus-group facility, the truth is you can do this kind of research yourself, and practically for free.

First, invite your patrons to a free lunch and show them your site, as well as several of your competitors' websites. Then, step back and listen to them talk. Do this one-on-one if you can, or in small groups.

Ask them some questions about what they like and don't like. Have them navigate basic areas of your site as you look on: Find out when the next performance is, or try to buy a ticket. You can even go so far as to design some new, improved web pages for your site to test out.

Ask them whether these new pages do a better job than your current pages. If you get your patrons talking to you directly and you listen to them and make changes based on their feedback, you can be sure that your website will be very effective.

What Is the Goal of Your Web Site?

If you take away only one principle from this chapter, it should be this: To build an effective website, you must have an overriding and specific goal. A clearly-articulated goal will help you make decisions.

Try to answer the following question in one sentence: What do you want your website to achieve?

The question seems rather simplistic, but it's amazing how many arts marketers can't answer this question. Without a clear definition of your objective, your site will be a missed marketing opportunity.

It's foolhardy to think that your website can be all things to all people. Yes, you can have many overlapping objectives. But from a marketing perspective, once you define the one goal that is most important for your website right now, you'll be able to direct your website's design and performance to achieve it. Your goal may change throughout the year, depending on whether you're selling tickets to a show, in the middle of a fundraising drive, or running an e-mail sign-up campaign, but make sure you're focused on one thing at a time. The clearer you are about your goal, the easier the job of designing your site will be.

Since we know users actually spend only a few minutes on each site they visit and view only a couple pages, your task will be translating your goal into a site design that produces the results you want.

Here's another question to ask yourself: *If you could guide each visitor to click on a single link on your site's main screen, what would it be?*

If you have a well-articulated goal, this should be easy to answer.

Make Your Goal Specific and Measurable

When we ask people, "What is the goal of your website?" we often get responses like these:

- "Sell tickets"

- "To inform the public about us, to actively engage their interest and curiosity"

- "A web presence that is inviting and informative"

- "Collect e-mails, donations, etc."

Those are all good things to aim for, but they don't offer any *measurable* benchmark by which to define success. Better-articulated goals would be:

- "We want to sell 55 percent of all our tickets online, because many of our colleagues achieve this rate. But our site now generates only about 19 percent of our ticket sales."

- "We know that the bulk of our visitors want event information, but right now it's buried in our site. We now have only 15 percent of our page views relating to the current show, and we want to raise that number to 50 percent."

- "We know that 70 percent of the people coming to our museum's site want to know what the special exhibition is. So we want to have at least 25 percent of our entire site traffic view the current-exhibition page."

Each of these answers demonstrates a very specific objective, along with a measurable goal that can be used as a benchmark for your design team and for later site analysis.

There is no doubt that building a great website is more complex than it seems. Because you have nearly infinite design freedom, much of the development process is subjective. And if you've got a group of people helping to make decisions, you run the risk of your site looking like it was designed by committee. We hope that these last two chapters have offered a useful structure for what is typically an unstructured, costly, and time-consuming site-design process, a structure that will help you not only build a great site, but also keep it on track to support your marketing objectives and connect with your patrons.

Next we will turn to e-commerce—which in our case has mostly to do with ticketing. Ticketing is the tangible evidence of your success in breaking the Fifth Wall—it means a patron responds to your marketing message and directly takes action by deciding to attend and buying a ticket.

Chapter 9

Online Ticketing Is Part of the Arts Experience

As you strive to break the Fifth Wall and bring patrons into your halls on a regular basis, you'll discover that the ticket-buying experience is actually a central component of building relationships with your audience. It's the moment when all of the cumulative effects of your marketing come together. It's what you've been striving for: to get patrons to transact with you and buy a ticket.

And, just as subject lines are the most important part of your e-mail newsletters, the ticket-purchase page is one of the most important areas on your website. It is there where the patron commits to a relationship with you, on their way to your cultural program.

To understand why the moment of ticket purchase is so important, consider the following question: When does a cultural event begin, and when does it end? For the traditionalists, the answer is simple. When the curtain goes up, it starts: when the curtain comes down, it's over.

There's another way of looking at it: The cultural event starts the moment a potential patron decides to attend. Once her decision is made, she takes action by making a call, visiting the box office, or going to your website. Each of these experiences results (theoretically) in a transaction—a ticket sale—which is the start of the cultural event.

If you accept this definition, then the website visit is *part of the arts experience*. The ticket purchase becomes the first (and most interactive) contact that your patron is likely to have with your organization before she walks into your venue.

Therefore, the online ticket-buying experience itself ought to be simple, professional, and smooth. The quality, ease, and manner of the e-commerce transaction set the tone for everything that follows. If you get this right, you create the expectation that everything else your organization has to offer will be good. Of course, the opposite is also true.

Before you continue reading, take a moment to go online and begin to buy a ticket on JetBlue.com. In our view, JetBlue does an excellent job selling a ticket. As of this writing, the site is clean, clear, and pleasant to use. From this initial interaction they begin to build your expectation for how things will go at the airport and on the plane. Clearly JetBlue understands that the beginning of your flight takes place on their website. In contrast, go to most other airlines' sites and try to do the same thing. You'll quickly see that they must have been built by their engineers and lawyers. They tend to be overly complicated, drab, and frustrating.

Given the upscale demographics of arts patrons, it stands to reason that your patrons have many online shopping experiences every month. In all likelihood, they regularly visit websites of retailers who spend millions of dollars to perfect the e-commerce experience. Your patrons expect quality, and you don't get a pass because you're a non-profit organization.

So what do we mean by a good buying experience? Here are a few key concepts that should guide the ticket-buying experience on your website:

Clarity

One of the most important aspects of any e-commerce experience is to make sure a buyer is absolutely clear about where he is in the process. If your ticket purchase requires three screens, make sure there's some indication on each page telling buyers what step they are on. Simple numbers can work ("Page 1 of 3"), or any kind of clear graphic, such as a progress bar. The more your patrons understand what's going on, the more comfortable they will be, and the more likely they are to complete the transaction.

Transparency

Make sure your patrons know what they are buying, how much it costs, and whether there are any additional fees, taxes, or add-ons. All fees and add-ons should be visible as early in the process as possible and certainly on the final shopping-cart page, before you ask people to enter their credit card information. No one has ever been faulted for full disclosure. But extras thrown in at the very end of a transaction will surely enrage even the most easygoing buyer.

Recently even Ticketmaster, a company not historically known for being friendly to consumers, has embraced a more transparent approach to the ticket-buying experience by displaying up-front the actual price of the ticket you're purchasing, including all of the fees that will be charged.

Simplicity

Many arts marketers believe that requiring customers to log in before buying a ticket online is a better idea than an anonymous purchase. We hear the following refrain regularly: "Why wouldn't we want to let our patrons sign in and manage their contact information and ticket purchases?"

Well, there is a downside to that approach. Some consumers find it irritating to be forced to create a username and password simply to make a one-time purchase. Just because they're buying a ticket from an arts organization doesn't mean they plan to do so on a regular basis in the future—they haven't made that kind of commitment yet.

If you sell mostly single tickets spread throughout the year, a log-in requirement creates an extra barrier for your patrons, and they may abandon the purchase entirely. The practicality of an online log-in may not make up for the hassle it creates; we're all in favor of collecting information about your patrons, but not at such a heavy cost.

This is not to say that customer log-ins don't have any utility at all. If your organization sells subscriptions, for example, it may be beneficial to offer your patrons a place to manage their subscriptions, exchange, renew them, or send in a customer inquiry online.

The bottom line is that the usefulness of the customer log-in varies directly with the frequency in which your patrons interact with your site. Build a customer log-in system if you really need it and if it will serve your audience, not simply because "the big organizations all do it."

Certainty

When someone completes an e-commerce transaction with you (whether a ticket purchase or a donation), you must send a confirmation e-mail immediately. Leaving out this crucial step will create a sense of distrust and confusion among your buyers. When a confirmation comes instantly, the message your buyer gets is that you run a tight operation and that their transaction was handled securely and professionally.

Consistency

Integrate your online ticket buying with the rest of your website. Do not banish your ticket buyers to Siberia, sending them off to a ticket vendor's site that looks nothing like yours. Maintaining your brand means extending the colors, language, and personality of your site into the ticket buying experience. As we noted earlier, this is an opportunity to show what it is like to be in a relationship with your organization.

If you have to send patrons off to a ticketing vendor's site to complete their purchase, this goal of consistency still applies. We encourage you to customize that ticketing page in whatever way the vendor allows. Can you upload a well-designed, attractive banner that incorporates the logo, colors, and personality of your website?

Totality

Patrons want to transact with you online for nearly *everything*. They want to buy single tickets, make reservations, give donations, buy subscriptions, renew their subscriptions, exchange tickets, upgrade tickets, and donate the tickets or send the tickets to others.

However, from our own research we know there's a demonstrable gap between what arts patrons want and what arts organizations currently provide. About 73 percent of the arts patrons we surveyed said they were interested in buying or renewing their subscriptions online. But only 36 percent indicated that they *have* actually bought or renewed a subscription online over the past year, because many organizations' sites don't have that option. It seems that the more online transaction opportunities you offer your patrons, the happier they will be. (And, of course, by driving more transactions online, you also cut down on the time staff are busy handling phone calls.)

We realize that many of the things we're talking about are sometimes outside your control. Most organizations work with vendors to provide web-based ticketing technology, and often cannot control all of the elements described above. Today many vendors *do* understand the importance of all of these functionalities, and are working toward making them available.

In conclusion, we hope it's clear that the ticketing experience is part of the process of breaking the Fifth Wall. Whether you do your own ticketing or work with a vendor, ensuring that your patrons have a good e-commerce experience is as important a component of your marketing plan as anything we've talked about thus far.

SECTION IV: Social Media

Chapter 10

Making Connections Personal

Social media, though a relatively recent phenomenon, has already changed the very nature of online communication. It has allowed people to connect with each other, and with organizations and brands, in a way that's simpler, less expensive, and more direct than anything that had come before.

Up to this point, this book has focused on how to adapt well-established technologies such as e-mail and websites to break the Fifth Wall. As a communication tool, social media requires no adaptation at all. It is itself the very definition of breaking the Fifth Wall.

Social media cuts out any sort of middleman by allowing instant access to online tools that create a one-to-one, unstructured, and authentic relationship in a way that no other marketing technique previously discussed does.

The highly personal, highly transparent nature of social media breaks down barriers between companies and consumers, between celebrities and fans; it can break down the barrier between your organization and your patrons as well. Imagine how connected patrons would feel to an arts organization that was as responsive and personable as a close friend.

For the patron, it's the difference between quietly watching a play on the stage, and engaging with all sorts of people as an active participant at a cocktail reception. In the age of social media, you can—metaphorically—carry your organization beyond the stage and participate in an ongoing conversation with your patrons in an entirely new and compelling way.

Our research shows that for patrons, this kind of personal connection with arts organizations is important. It's more than just a nice add-on to the arts experience; feeling connected is valuable in itself. Seventy-four percent of the arts patrons we surveyed said that it *matters* to them to feel that an arts organization knows them personally. Fifty percent admitted that feeling like an arts organization knew them personally would influence them to attend that organization's events more often. And 71 percent of those who follow an arts organization on Facebook or Twitter stated they feel more connected as a result.

I—Michelle—am taking the lead on this chapter. I have worked at Patron Technology for six years now, and in that time I've experienced the era of social media from two sides: as a participant, of course (I've had a Facebook profile since August 2004); and as a professional working in the field of arts marketing and building technology for arts organizations. Everything I'll mention in this section emerges from a combination of these two perspectives.

In general, social media offers you the opportunity to move beyond mass marketing and foster personal relationships with your patrons. A caveat, though: Social media also affords numerous opportunities to inadvertently sabotage those relationships and damage your brand, if not used properly. In this section, I'll help you navigate the social media landscape carefully and successfully.

I will focus principally on Facebook and Twitter, the two leading social media sites *of the moment*. Things change fast in the world of social media, and as a result, certain parts of this chapter may seem out of date by the time you read this. But bear in mind, *social media itself is not a fad*. Rather, social media on the web is a new means for achieving very old goals: communicating among friends and building community.

Given the way social media ties into our very nature, it's no wonder sites like Facebook and Twitter have been so widely adopted. The idea is here to stay.

Though today I'll be writing about Facebook and Twitter, who's to know what might be on the rise a year from now? Because of that, the tips and examples in the next chapter will refer to these two platforms, but only as specific examples of universal concepts. Even if Facebook becomes yesterday's news, the basic philosophies and techniques you read about here will still hold true.

Social Media by the Numbers

Social media represents a fundamental shift in the way people behave and participate online.

Let's look at some numbers that clearly demonstrate this. Facebook is by far the largest social media website. As of early 2011, Facebook had over 550 million active users. About 140 million of those are in the U.S., out of a total population of just over 300 million.[6] As a reference point, *The New York Times* has only about 1 million subscribers, and *Sports Illustrated* has about 3.5 million.[7]

Since Twitter launched in 2006, more than 165 million accounts have been registered. While the number of *active* accounts on Twitter is a good deal lower than that, the platform has experienced enormous growth over the past several years, and is clearly the second most influential social media property in the U.S.

At this point, it's a good bet that a large segment of your audience is using at least one of these sites—no matter the demographic makeup of your patrons. Indeed, we should debunk the myth that social media is used only by young people. While it's true that Facebook *began* as a site for college students, for years the fastest growing age group on Facebook has been the 55-and-older group. That age bracket grew *923 percent in 2009 alone.*[8]

Fifty percent of our own arts survey respondents said they visit Facebook at least once a week; of that group, 67 percent said they had visited an arts organization's Facebook Page during the previous month. Looking at just the under-35 age group, 39 percent of them reported they follow an arts organization on Facebook, and 10 percent said they follow arts organizations on both Facebook and Twitter.

Facebook and Twitter: A Short Overview

While social media has been widely adopted by the general public, the arts industry's use of it has been varied and inconsistent. Some arts marketers are active users; others are still tentative and perhaps not certain what these sites can do for them. There are plenty of resources out there for those who want to understand the details—*Facebook for Dummies* and *Twitter for Dummies* are great places to start. We've also compiled further resources at www.fifthwall.com. Below, I have set out the basic terms and information that every arts marketer ought to know. (If you're an "advanced" social media user, you may want to skip ahead to Chapter 11.)

Facebook

While Facebook began as a site for college students and recent graduates to connect with each other, it has grown exponentially and its user base now comprises an enormous variety of people. But Facebook does not consist only of individuals. A few years ago, Facebook created "Pages" in response to the growing desire of organizations and businesses to have a presence on the site. Pages are devoted to this purpose, and creating a Facebook Page is the most effective way to represent your arts organization on Facebook.

Your Facebook Page will include your organization's contact information, your website URL, and probably a list of upcoming events. Most importantly, you can post messages to the site using your Page, just like an individual can. Those posts appear in the News Feed of all your "Fans" (those patrons who choose to "friend" or "like" your organization on Facebook), right alongside posts from their friends.

Twitter

Twitter is also a platform that enables people to communicate online, but in a slightly different way. Twitter strips down the social media experience to its essence. From your Twitter account, you can post short messages of just 140 characters or less. Those messages are called "tweets," and can be read by the public or by others with Twitter accounts who have specifically chosen to "follow" a particular user.

Using Twitter is a little like sending out a text message, but to all of your friends at once.

Twitter users can publicly reply to and refer to each other in their posts by placing an "@" in front of a username:

Michelle hey @Allison, are you going to see In the Heights any time this month?
10 minutes ago via web

Allison @Michelle I'm going to wait and see it right before it closes..sniffsniff...but i think @Lily is going with her mom next week
6 minutes ago via web in reply to Michelle

You'll also frequently see the letters "RT" preceding a username on a Twitter post. RT stands for "retweet" and it simply means that one user is quoting another, re-posting what someone else said, sometimes with added commentary.

Michelle i totally agree: RT @Allison waffles are so much better than pancakes!
4 minutes ago via web

These are the basic facts and terms to be familiar with. Ultimately, in order to use social media successfully for your organization, you need to be comfortable using it for yourself. You wouldn't try to coach a baseball team if you'd never even been on a ball field before. How could you understand the rules of the game or the culture of the team if you hadn't experienced it firsthand? The same goes for anyone at your organization who's going to be involved in your social media efforts. If you're convinced that social media is an outlet worth exploring for your organization, I recommend signing up and getting involved on a personal level first. Only then will you be ready to take the next steps to social media success.

Chapter 11

Social Media Success

What does social media success look like? It's more than just setting up a Facebook Page and waiting for magic to happen. When you're using social media well, you'll be energizing and exciting your patrons by sharing insider information and creating great content, making personal connections by communicating directly with individuals, and doing all this in an organized, coordinated way.

Content, communication, and coordination are the pillars of social media success. Get these things right, and you'll get great results.

CONTENT

At the same time that social media sites have enabled more direct communication between people and brands, they have also created an enormous amount of content for people to read each day. It used to be the case that the "news" was something you found in a newspaper. Today, reading the news often means reading the news *feed*, and people are keeping up not only with traditional news sources but also with constant updates about their friends as well. With that much more information out there for people to take in, standing out and rising above the din is the biggest challenge for organizations creating a social media presence. That's why, just like with your e-mail newsletters, the first step to succeeding with social media is simply to have great content.

When in doubt, don't think like a marketer

It's easy to fall into the trap of thinking of social media as hyper-direct marketing. After all, you have the power to communicate with people on a close personal level, and they've all chosen to follow you—isn't that an opportunity for targeted marketing to the nth degree?

But here's the catch: Your patrons don't see Twitter and Facebook as marketing channels, and just because they want to connect with you doesn't mean they're opting in to receive *marketing* communications from you, as they do when they join your e-mail list. Facebook was created for person-to-person communication.

Instead, you need to consider your presence in your fans' news feeds as a privilege. Make sure you continually justify your presence by being worthwhile, relevant, and engaging—and appropriate to the medium.

Here's an example of how that might look:

The Winterthur Museum is clearly promoting its events, but without sounding like an advertisement. When they write about that "glorious burst of color," of course, what they really mean is, "You should come see it." But they took off their marketing hat for this post, and rather than explicitly trying to make a sale, they simply expressed their enthusiasm about their museum.

Unfortunately, there are plenty of examples of what NOT to do. This one is made up, but it's representative of the postings I see on Facebook every day:

Laboratory Theatre wants you to come see Savion Glover this weekend, March 13-14-15, at 8pm, $20!!!!
2 seconds ago · Comment · Like

When I see a message like that in my own News Feed, I scroll right past. It doesn't even register. Compare that message to this one from ArtPride New Jersey's "Discover Jersey Arts" program:

Discover Jersey Arts How does a 55-piece orchestra sound to you? NJ State Opera's 75th Anniversary Production The Gershwins' "Porgy & Bess" is coming soon. Special Group Rate of 20% off will be offered to all DJA members. Visit the event page for more information on this loud, live event.

JerseyArts.com Event Detail - New Jersey State Opera's 75th Anniversary Production The Gershwins' "P
www.jerseyarts.com
The NJ State Opera presents the Newark premiere of the Gershwin's great American masterwork and jazz opera, Porgy and Bess, directed by Jonathan Eaton and conducted by Jason Tramm. Accompanied by the NJSOpera Orchestra and Chorus the all star cast featuring GREGG BAKER, LAQUITA MITCHELL, LESTER LYN...

Yesterday at 10:40am · Comment · Like · Share

It is not drastically different; it still says, "Buy these tickets." But this version offers a little more for the reader to grab on to. It asks a question! It says that there's a 55-piece orchestra, and it will be a "loud, live event"— already that's more intriguing than a statement of the fact that a show exists.

Using social media to promote your events is fine, but do more than just announce them. Post clips of past performances, post a picture of the stage or the dressing room, post a link to a great review—build excitement by offering your patrons a glimpse of the experience itself, making the event something real, something more than a line on the calendar.

Look who's talking

Who is the voice of your social media account? Who "speaks" for your organization on your social media page? This choice influences so much of the content you post.

Should you personify your organization, talking about what "we" have going on this week? Or is your organization's voice a specific person, such as the executive director or marketing director speaking on the organization's behalf? What pronouns do you use? Is the tone casual, like chatting with a friend, or does it sound more like you're quoting your season brochure or mission statement?

There's no particular best practice for making this decision—what matters is that you decide, that you remain consistent, and that whatever you choose, it's something that feels natural.

Our own Patron Technology Twitter account is @patrontcs. It's run by our Client Services Department, and even though the actual postings are written almost exclusively by one person, the account always refers to the company as "we," and the posts are primarily directed at current clients, not prospective ones. These are decisions we reached after careful consideration, and the tone and feel of the voice account for our company.

Some arts organizations have taken a decidedly creative approach to establishing their voice on Twitter. At the American Museum of Natural History, a giant model of a blue whale hangs from the ceiling in the main hall of ocean and marine life. All the tweets from the "@

NatHistoryWhale" account about goings-on at the museum are from the whale's perspective, who also sprinkles in some whale-related news and articles.

> New research suggests multiple types of Orca "Killer Whales" http://is.gd/bIE79 Hurray biodiversity!!
>
> 1:01 PM Apr 26th via web
> Retweeted by 5 people
>
> NatHistoryWhale

> Had another school group in today. One girl threw a paper airplane that almost landed on my tail. :)
>
> 2:14 PM Oct 26th via web
> Retweeted by 2 people
>
> NatHistoryWhale

Vancouver Opera maintains several different Twitter accounts. The main account gets updated several times a week and speaks for the whole organization. But they also have several specialized accounts dedicated to their more creative endeavors. They've created a character, @OperaNinja, who live-tweets during dress rehearsals. The "ninja" part of the name defines the persona:

> Just been asked to turn off all electronic devices - but the OperaNinja follows no orders!
>
> 11:00 PM Apr 22nd via TweetDeck
>
> operaninja
> Opera Ninja

> The string section is waving their sticks hello. Note to self: violin sticks would make a good ninja weapon should I need to fight.
> 1:09 AM Apr 23rd via TweetDeck
>
>
> operaninja
> Opera Ninja

> I know I am supposed to be moved by the Countess' sorrow, but mostly I just want her dress. It's black and gorgeous and fit for a ninja.
> 1:33 AM Apr 23rd via TweetDeck
>
> operaninja
> Opera Ninja

The Ninja tweets about every opera in their season, as a way of introducing the work and drawing in new patrons. The Opera Ninja is actually run by a rotating group of staff members and bloggers, but everyone adopts the same tone for the character.

Let others speak for you!

Social media isn't just about writing your own posts and creating your own content. A powerful element of social media culture is about sharing information and linking to others' content. Facebook's own statistics document that more than 30 billion pieces of content are shared among users on the site each month.

This means that your presence in the social space is enhanced the more you gather up interesting and relevant links from around the web to share with your users. This could mean something as straightforward as posting a review of your show:

Abingdon Theatre Company ENGAGING SHAW is starting to get noticed in the press! (We're on BroadwayWorld and Theatermania, too!)

Abingdon Theatre Company to Present Real-Life Shavian Romance, Engaging Shaw; Cast Announced - Playb
www.playbill.com
Off-Broadway's Abingdon Theatre Company will present the New York City premiere of John Morogiello's Engaging Shaw, a play about the unlikely but true relationship between playwright George Bernard Shaw and wealthy socialite Charlotte Payne-Townshend.

2 hours ago · Comment · Like · Share

Or an article that features your performers:

American Ballet Theatre Check out dancers from American Ballet Theatre in ballet-inspired
bridal fashions from the Spring issue of Martha Stewart Weddings.

Ballet-Inspired Bridal Fashion
www.marthastewartweddings.com
Bridal fashion and styles inspired by the ballet. From tutus to tulle to ballet pink, this is as feminine and romantic as they come.

about an hour ago · Comment · Like · Share

53 people like this.

View all 9 comments

It doesn't have to stop there. What else can you find that would interest your fans and followers? This link from the Public Theater isn't directly related to their current programming, but Jonathan Groff performed at the Public in the past:

PU **The Public Theater** Watch Public Theater alum Jonathan Groff on GLEE! **Hide**
Season premiere tomorrow night. What a cutie!

Those You've Known: Lea Michele and Jonathan Groff Reunite on 'Glee' - ArtsBeat Blog - NYTimes.com
artsbeat.blogs.nytimes.com
The "Spring Awakening" stars find themselves as romantic rivals on "Glee," and talk about their unusual but enduring friendship.

3 hours ago · Comment · Like · Share

and 6 others like this.

I LOVE JG!!!!!!!!!!!!!!!!!
3 hours ago

Already saw it- and he's SO GOOD in it!!!
3 hours ago

Write a comment...

Not only has the theatre taken advantage of a pop-culture moment (Jon Groff on *Glee*) and made it relevant to their organization, they've also made their organization a conduit within the social and personal world of their patrons. From the excited comments below the post, we can see they have indeed engaged their fans.

COMMUNICATION

All this emphasis on the importance of great content can start to make social media marketing feel overwhelming. The idea of adding hours and hours of content-creation and content-finding to an already heavy workload could scare you off social media entirely—who has time for all that?

Creating a successful social media presence can be time-consuming, but—and here's the good news—it doesn't have to rely on constantly posting new content.

Social media can be useful for disseminating information quickly, but the key word is "social"—the main function of these platforms is to create relationships. Don't think of Facebook and Twitter only as broadcast channels; rather, focus on them as communication tools.

Start a conversation

Ask questions, request feedback, encourage participation, provoke discussion! If you can get your fans and followers to chime in, you're creating an environment where they can connect with each other, not just with you. (And their conversations count as content, too.)

Here's an example from the Antaeus Company's Facebook Page. They managed to get a whole group of fans posting responses:

The Antaeus Company OK, we want to see how quickly our Fans can post Romeo and Juliet, line by line, without peeking. To begin: Prologue Two households, both alike in dignity
April 19 at 12:41am · Comment · Like

 in fair Verona where we lay our scene.
April 19 at 12:45am · Report

 From ancient grudge, break to new mutiny,
April 19 at 12:53am · Report

 from ancient grudge break to new mutiny
April 19 at 12:53am · Report

 where civil blood makes civil hands unclean
April 19 at 12:55am · Report

 From forth the fatal loins of these two foes…
April 19 at 8:40am · Delete

A pair of star crossed lovers take their life
April 19 at 9:14am · Report

Whose misadventured piteous overthrows..
April 19 at 10:55am · Report

Do with their death bury their parents' strife.
April 19 at 12:22pm · Report

the fearful passage of their death marked love…
April 19 at 12:32pm · Report

And the continuance of their parents' rage,
April 19 at 5:07pm · Report

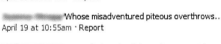

The initial post took no more than a minute, yet it drove a conversation that went on for the entire day. Even though this is far from traditional marketing, it's both strategic and completely on-topic. Antaeus's upcoming show was *King Lear*, so they found a way to get people in a Shakespearean mood.

Here's an example from outside the arts world: The Discovery Channel frequently checks in with their fans the day after a TV show airs to ask what they thought of it:

The comment thread goes on and on, as the posters debate about the start of the new season. There's no reason a post like this couldn't work for an arts organization.

The conversation you start doesn't have to be about your own organization, either. Below, Pilobolus Dance Theater found a fantastic photo of a graceful, dancer-like baseball player (Tim Lincecum, who happens to now be a 2010 World Series champion), and shared it with their fans:

This is a thought-provoking observation, and it got their fans talking with each other about athleticism of all kinds.

Join the conversation

Perhaps the most compelling reason to develop a social media presence is that your social media presence may already exist even without your knowing it. If you've ever Googled yourself, you know that the Internet is full of information that you might not even have known was there.

Take a moment and visit http://search.twitter.com. Type in the name of your organization or venue. You may be surprised to see what comes up.

If people are out there tweeting about your organization, you will see it by searching. And if so, you should be part of that conversation. As we demonstrated earlier, arts patrons value a personal connection with your organizations—this is an opportunity to let them know you're listening, and offer some personal attention.

Here's a non-arts example that shows how easy it is to be friendly and welcoming on Twitter:

My friend Jon runs a big Harry Potter fan club in New York. The group was having a meeting at Café Metro, a chain of sandwich shops in the city, and he tweeted this message about the group's plans:

RT @   Reminder: "September Meetup - Half-Blood Prince Discussion" is tomorrow, Thursday, September 3, 2009 7:00 PM @cafemetro
about 1 hour ago from TweetDeck

Café Metro is on Twitter too, and they were listening. Right after Jon posted the message above, he received this reply:

CafeMetro @   Hey Jon RT this to the group: @CAFEMETRO WELCOMES THE 1/2 BLOOD PRINCE GROUP THIS THURSDAY! ENJOY THE DISCUSSION AND FOOD!
about 1 hour ago from web in reply to

109

All they did was take a moment to let the group know they were listening and that they appreciated the business. By welcoming the group, the restaurant became more than just an invisible backdrop for the meeting, it became a friend.

You have an even easier opportunity to be responsive when people ask you questions directly. For this reason, make sure you present your Facebook Page or Twitter account as a place where people can get answers quickly.

The American Ballet Theatre has over 100,000 Facebook fans, and I don't doubt that their commitment to replying to comments and questions on their Page is a significant factor contributing to their success.

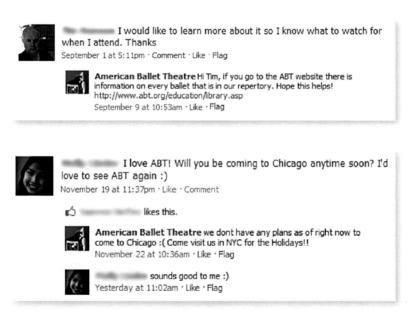

Here's one of my favorite examples of how an organization successfully used social media for customer service. It happens to be one that's pretty close to home, because it involves a Twitter conversation between my co-worker Lily and the Theatre Development Fund (TDF).

TDF offers discount tickets to their members, and they have an active Twitter presence where they monitor what people are saying about them. When Lily posted on Twitter saying that she wanted to buy tickets for a particular performance of *Next to Normal* on Broadway, referring to TDF by name, they noticed and replied.

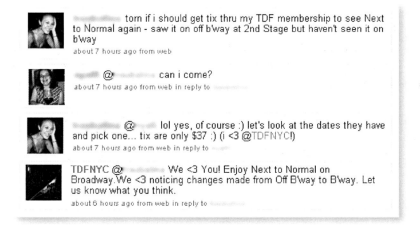

If that were the end of the story, I would already consider it both a social media success and an example of great customer service.

But the story continues. Lily ended up having trouble getting tickets for the show she wanted, and she posted about that too:

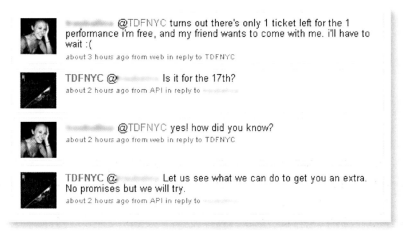

About an hour later, Lily got a call—yes, a real phone call—from TDF, saying, "Hey, we've got your two tickets to *Next to Normal* on the 17th."

That is customer service on a whole new level, customer service before the customer even realizes she needs service! They saw Lily's post saying she likes them; they saw that she was having a problem; they looked her up in their database and decided that they would try to help fix the problem. This gets at the real value of social media: the one-on-one conversation and relationship-building that would have been impossible even five years ago.

There are many organizations and brands out there that don't reply to people at all, and they are missing the whole point of Twitter. That doesn't mean you need to go around handing out tickets to everyone—TDF certainly went above and beyond—but these instant mini-conversations with people are what Twitter is all about. Its best use isn't as a broadcast system. If you're not replying to people, you're missing an incredible opportunity to break the Fifth Wall.[9]

COORDINATION

Creating a plan for building content and then effectively communicating with social media requires coordinating effort across departments. Your social media marketing might have a more casual tone than some of your other marketing efforts, but that doesn't mean that it can be approached casually. It's still important to have a structured approach in place. These are the nuts and bolts of getting your program off the ground.

Distinguish between strategy and execution

An arts organization's social media efforts usually live in the marketing department, but there will be—and should be!—crossover with other departments in the organization. There's certainly an element of PR to any social media usage, and the development department should stay involved as well. Indeed, if social media is a real-time mouthpiece for your organization, then all departments that have touch points with your customers should be involved. Just make sure that all these pieces come together and that ultimately, there's one person leading the charge.

Of course, having a single point of execution will mean different things depending on the size of your organization. Organizations with a multi-million-dollar budget or 30 or more employees might invest in a Director of Social Media—as many forward-thinking arts organizations now have done. This person would manage your social media presence across departments: collecting content, aligning messages, and making sure that there's a consistent tone in all your social communications.

For smaller organizations, it may be impossible to create a full-time position just for social media. But a mistake that many organizations make is handing off the entirety of their social media work to an intern or volunteer. "Hey, she's 19 and chatting with her friends on Facebook twenty-four hours a day. She must be an expert!" I've been flabbergasted to see job postings from organizations seeking a social media manager as a part-time, work-from-home position.

It should be easy to see why this attitude is fraught with problems. The person in charge of your social media is creating a public face of your organization. You want to make sure that your organization is well represented, and that's not a job to hand off to someone who's not fully involved.

That's not to say there's no place for an intern or volunteer in this process at all. As long as you have a clear leader in charge of creating the overall message and managing the process, you can make a distinction between strategizing and executing the day-to-day work. Find an enthusiastic intern or volunteer to be the person who actually posts on Facebook daily—just make sure that there's plenty of oversight, and that she's not the real decision-maker.

Measure your success

Given the way social media works, it's clear that your goals and metrics for your social media efforts aren't going to look like the ones you might use for other types of marketing. In the world of e-mail marketing, we obsess over metrics: open rates! click rates! A/B testing! ROI! But those ideas don't translate well into social media.

At this stage of the development of social media, there aren't many globally standardized and accepted benchmarks. Creating your social media marketing plan will largely begin with experimentation—finding out what works and what doesn't work for your audience. When you're experimenting, you absolutely have to track and measure what you're doing, so you can establish your *own* benchmarks.

There's a seemingly endless list of things you could be tracking. To create a finite sense of them, I've listed below four categories of metrics to gauge. (Visit fifthwall.com for more details about how to gather this data.)

1. INTEREST: At the most basic level, "interest" gauges whether your audience is responding to what you're putting out there: Are you posting content that people want to see? Are you offering something that they can't find elsewhere?

Things to track: total number of fans on Facebook, total number of followers on Twitter, click-through rate per post.

2. ENGAGEMENT: "Engagement" is the social aspect of social media—not just getting people to pay attention, but encouraging them to respond. Are you presenting your organization in a friendly, welcoming way that makes patrons want to talk to you?

Things to track: number of weekly comments on Facebook, number of weekly @replies on Twitter.

3. REACH: "Reach" is a measure of how far your messages extend beyond your own social media site. Are your fans and followers so excited by what you have to say that they're re-posting your messages for all of their friends to see? The term "going viral" refers to content whose popularity multiplies when people continue to pass it along to more and more friends.

Things to track: number of shares and retweets, percent of your posts that get shared or retweeted.

4. IMPACT: "Impact" is what it all comes down to, what your boss or board members want to hear when they ask, "Why are we bothering with social media?" Are your social media efforts having a measurable effect on website traffic, ticket sales, or donations?

Things to track: percent of tickets sold online, weekly or monthly page views on your website, and where that traffic is coming from.

All of these things are easy to measure, and it doesn't have to take more than a spreadsheet to do it. There are plenty of applications (from Google Analytics to Facebook's "Insights" section to other external services) that can help you gather the data. Finding your own benchmarks is the first step to turning social media into a bona-fide marketing tool. Once you have them, you can create goals, and strategies to reach them.

Set a goal, and start testing what works and what doesn't. What happens when you tweet at 9:00 AM instead of 11:00 AM? Do you get more comments when you post photos, or with text only? If you currently sell 45 percent of your tickets online, can social media help you increase that number to 60 percent? There are no hard-and-fast best practices here, but you should have no trouble figuring out the best practices for your own organization. See what your patrons respond to, and then give them what they want.

Again—no single metric will tell the whole story, and some of what you're doing may only be proven anecdotally. Social media marketing is part of an overall process of breaking the Fifth Wall and connecting with your audience after they leave your theatre. That engagement may happen while enticing a sale, asking patrons about the experience after a performance, doing customer service, or connecting patrons with others who have similar arts interests. All of these things go along with an actual ticket purchase, but they aren't necessarily the key drivers of it.

Social Media on a Tight Schedule

Be wary of anything that looks like an amazing shortcut in the world of social media marketing. Like with anything else, if you want to succeed, you need to commit to making time to get it right. A full-time social media coordinator may be the ideal, but you can still get plenty of value from social media in smaller chunks of time. As a guide, here's what I consider to be the bare minimum of what every organization should be doing on Facebook and Twitter. This minimal approach is meant to help you get started. I have designed a set of work schedules to show you that even a very small investment of time is more valuable than sitting on the sidelines.

Facebook:

> **Weekly:** Plan a week of content in advance. (This should sound familiar—it's the same advice we give about e-mail newsletters.) Leave room in the schedule for new of-the-moment links or announcements that arise during the week.

> **A few times a week:** Post a new link, photo, or status update.

> **Daily:** Check in to see if there are comments needing responses or questions to answer.

If your Page is wildly popular and you have dozens of comments to follow up on every day… well, then you're doing something right. Be thrilled that Facebook now takes more time to manage, and go mine your community for a volunteer to help.

Twitter:

> **Weekly:** Plan your content in advance if you can. Write a few tweets up front and have them ready to go.

> **Daily:** Send your tweets! Remember that the Twitter stream moves quickly. If you allocate 15 minutes per day to Twitter, don't lump all those minutes together. Spread out your posts so they

don't get lost or ignored. It's easy to tell when an organization has reserved a specific time of the day for Twitter. You'll see 15 posts in a row from 11 to 11:15 AM, and then nothing for the rest of the day. It's better to tweet a few times during the day, which is more in keeping with the conversational tone of Twitter.

Resist the urge to link your Facebook and Twitter accounts, feeding content directly from one to the other. There are all sorts of apps that let you do that easily, but remember: Beware of shortcuts. There will certainly be times when you want a similar—or even identical—message posted to both your Facebook and Twitter accounts, but don't automatically cross post everything. At least a handful of patrons will follow you on both. In our own survey, only 1 percent of patrons said they follow any organizations on Twitter only—but 10 percent said they follow organizations on both platforms. No matter how exciting and interesting your posts are, no one wants to read everything twice! At best, it can be confusing. At worst, you'll annoy people and dilute your message.

CREATIVITY

Social media is an opportunity for creativity and innovation. We've already seen some examples of organizations embracing the creative aspects of social media, with the Natural History whale and Vancouver's Opera Ninja. They're fun and engaging, and don't require an extra cent of your marketing budget.

Arts organizations are in an exceptionally good position to get creative with social media—because you have creative people working for you. Try something new! Try something weird! Come up with new ways to bring your art into the social media space.

Dance Theater Workshop: "Community Choreography"

Dance Theater Workshop's mission is to identify, present, and support independent contemporary artists and companies to advance dance and live performance in New York and worldwide. In 2010, Dance Theater

Workshop merged with Bill T. Jones/Arnie Zane Dance Company to become New York Live Arts.[10] Known for innovative programming, Dance Theater Workshop has also continually pushed the boundaries of marketing strategies.

From May 2009 to August 2010, Dance Theater Workshop created "Twitter Community Choreography," an open-source dance-video experiment. Using the organization's Twitter account (@DanceTWorkshop), a staff member would solicit short, simple movement instructions from followers that would then be interpreted by a performer and filmed.

Last call for Community Choreography 10! Tweet moves & tag them #cc10. This week's challenge: actual dance moves. (Ex. http://ow.ly/hOd4)

4:17 PM Jul 21st from HootSuite

DanceTWorkshop
Dance TheaterWorkshop

TDFNYC @DanceTWorkshop Sychronized swimming scissor kicks.
5:20 PM Aug 4th from API in reply to DanceTWorkshop

high5tix @DanceTWorkshop Progressively worse hand-cramping (movement from H5's day - *sigh*) #CC11
4:45 PM Aug 4th from web in reply to DanceTWorkshop

▬▬▬▬ @DanceTWorkshop #cc11 swing your arms around so that you don't fall backwards
4:33 PM Aug 4th from TwitterGadget

nyneofuturists @DanceTWorkshop #cc11 shimy
4:33 PM Aug 4th from web

▬▬▬▬ @DanceTWorkshop #cc11 Arrest yourself.
4:21 PM Aug 4th from web

▬▬▬▬ @DanceTWorkshop #cc11 do Kirk Gibson rounding the bases.
4:06 PM Aug 4th from TweetDeck

GMPP @DanceTWorkshop #cc11 put your hair in front of your face
3:59 PM Aug 4th from TweetDeck

The results of the community dance videos were shared on Twitter via YouTube and posted on Dance Theater Workshop's blog. The 22 videos were often surreal, nonsensical, even dadaist, and were crafted by a group of people ranging from non-dance tweeters to professional dancers and choreographers.

spin counterclockwise with right index finger pointing in the air.

As a result of Twitter Community Choreography, Dance Theater Workshop's Twitter followers and mailing-list subscribers grew. Dance Theater Workshop became one of the arts organizations to know about on Twitter, and that buzz and extended reach were contributing factors to Dance Theater Workshop's highest-selling season to date.

National Symphony Orchestra at Wolf Trap:
Live-Tweeted Program Notes

The NSO performs a series of outdoor summer concerts at Wolf Trap. For one performance of Beethoven's Pastoral Symphony, they decided that in addition to providing traditional program notes about the piece, they would "live-tweet" the notes to the audience as the concert was happening—sort of like "Pop-Up Video" for a symphony. So they had the conductor write up a series of 140-character-long notes about specific parts of the piece, set up a dedicated "cellphones-on" section out on the lawn, and posted the tweets in time with the part of the music they referred to.

Welcome to the @NSOatWolfTrap real time program note stream for
Thursday July 30 Beethoven Pastoral Symphony!
9:13 PM Jul 30th from TweetDeck

Beethoven was known for his long walks in the country to look for
inspiration. The 6th is a reflection of his emotions during his walks.
9:15 PM Jul 30th from TweetDeck

The symphony begins in the middle of a journey. The music evokes
singing birds, the sounds of a stream, and wheels on cobblestones.
9:26 PM Jul 30th from TweetDeck

We have arrived! Beethoven's joy of being in his countryside paradise is
expressed in its most emotional version here.
9:31 PM Jul 30th from TweetDeck

We find ourselves next to a peaceful brook. Inspiration for this movement
comes from a stream in Dornbach, near Beethoven's country home.
9:35 PM Jul 30th from TweetDeck

As the notes get quicker, the stream moves faster. Beethoven said that
as the tones get lower the water becomes deeper.
9:39 PM Jul 30th from TweetDeck

The orchestral birds have a conversation. The color of the flute and oboe
are important to Beethoven even tho he was deaf when he wrote this
9:40 PM Jul 30th from TweetDeck

Beethoven writes the music off a beat on purpose so it sounds like the
country band is not that good – or maybe a little drunk...
9:48 PM Jul 30th from TweetDeck

Suddenly the sound of distant thunder is heard – the violins make the
sound of raindrops.
9:52 PM Jul 30th from TweetDeck

A DOWNPOUR!
9:52 PM Jul 30th from TweetDeck

Beethoven adds trombones for the first time in the piece to add to the
sound of the sky opening up and the terrifying thunder.
9:54 PM Jul 30th from TweetDeck

The intention was to make the event more accessible to a wider
audience of people who might not be familiar with classical music. The
organization considered the experiment a success. According to a recap
post on the NSO blog:

> "We got a lot of press for this… But more importantly we opened
> up a world of music to young first-time future music lovers."[11]

Conclusion

The world keeps changing. In an age of mobile technology and ubiquitous connectivity, it's more important than ever to reach people in a personal, direct way, so that those connections don't seem like *marketing* at all. Amid these changes, social media will be the strongest, most effective tool you have to match the way the world is moving. It's the most natural means of breaking the Fifth Wall.

Adapting your organization to fit the paradigm of social media will, in the end, inform and influence every kind of marketing you do. Building relationships and connecting with your patrons are goals to strive for across your entire organization. In time, the lessons from this chapter will likely expand well beyond the narrow "social media" niche of marketing and begin to affect all the interactions you have with your patrons; the radical personalization that social media allows may become just as important in your e-mail and web marketing over the next decade.

SECTION V: CRM

Chapter 12

The CRM Advantage

We now depart from our discussion of how Internet marketing tools can help you break the Fifth Wall and reach patrons more effectively. This chapter focuses on how the Internet is also about to transform *back-office* technology for arts organizations and help you become a more customer-focused organization using Customer Relationship Management (CRM). CRM is both a new approach to managing your organization's relationship with your patrons and the technology that makes it possible.

Let's start with a big fat claim.

The adoption of Customer Relationship Management systems will create a *revolutionary* change for the arts and culture world.

With CRM, arts organizations will be more efficient and more effective, and arts managers will run more professional and productive operations.

The Problem That CRM Solves

Today most arts organizations are hampered by the technology used to run their businesses. Invariably, it is outdated and conceptually flawed.

Does this look like your organization?

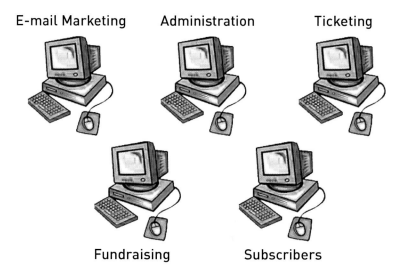

| E-mail Marketing | Administration | Ticketing |

| Fundraising | Subscribers |

Most of our clients have an office full of PCs. Each of these PCs is running one or more "transactional systems."

These transactional systems are:

- Stand-alone: Software programs and all data are stored on a local computer, and are accessible only to the person using that machine.

- Operation-oriented: The software is designed to help the user complete specific tasks in an efficient manner. It might be processing a donation or completing a ticket sale, but these systems are designed for efficiency in doing one thing.

- Department-focused: These programs are meant to help a single department run better. The development department has donation software; the marketing department has e-mail systems; and the box office runs ticketing software. The systems are not designed to interact or even share functionality or data.

For some years these kinds of systems represented the state of the art for business technology. But in today's world, they are not good enough. Their fundamental shortcoming is that while these stand-alone transactional systems help departments and individuals work more efficiently, none of them was designed to optimize communication with a patron!

The problems created by disconnected systems are many. We'll examine them here by imagining a fictitious patron—Shannon—who has several different types of interactions and transactions with an arts organization she attends. Over a five-year period, she receives newsletters from the organization's e-mail marketing system, makes donations that get recorded in the fundraising database and accounting software, and is a subscriber and single-ticket buyer.

The problem is, all this transactional information is scattered across five different computers in the office. And since those five systems don't talk to each other, Shannon's data can't be aggregated. To the staff working on fundraising appeals or renewal campaigns, she might as well be five different people.

With systems like these, you never have a 360-degree view of any one patron. And if you can't know everything about Shannon at a glance, it's going to be that much harder to break the Fifth Wall and truly connect with her.

These systems cause difficulties on a larger, organization-wide scale, too. Without aggregated data, it's impossible to get meaningful reports that can help you run your organization. Sure, the box office manager might be satisfied with the ticketing reports, and the development director is an expert at using the specialized fundraising software. But what about the executive director who needs to prepare for a strategic planning meeting with the board? Is it possible to easily generate a report of all of the people buying tickets over the past six weeks who also donated more than $100 over the past six months? Unlikely. Gathering information like that requires an integrated system, not separate transactional ones.

The Evolution of Arts Technology

How did we get into this mess? In and of themselves, there's nothing wrong with transactional systems. They are the result of decades of evolution in back-office technology beginning in the 1950s, when the field of arts marketing and management was just developing. Before computers, all of the records for the box office, accounting, development, and other departmental activities were kept in paper ledgers and notebooks. This was the world where the box office really had tickets stored in little boxes!

In the 1960s, mainframe computing arrived to serve the corporate world, starting the march toward greater and greater efficiencies powered by ever-expanding computational power. First-generation mainframe computers were located in specially cooled data centers, usually in basements. Workers accessed them from their desks through "dumb terminals" connected to the mainframe. These systems offered employees access to new software tools, including digitally editable documents and spreadsheets. Mainframes were great if you happened to work for a Fortune 500 company that could afford them. If not, you were left sitting on the technological sideline.

When the PC arrived in the 1980s, it was both the best and the worst thing ever to happen to small businesses. The PC democratized computing technology, and suddenly a small business could do the same type of word processing as the big corporations. More important, Microsoft Excel (which was the successor to programs like VisiCalc and Lotus 1-2-3) changed forever the way office workers managed their day-to-day operations. PC-based systems began to automate the development department, where fundraising could run faster and better. The same happened at the box office and in the accounting department. As everything moved from analog to digital, everyone's efficiency shot up.

But what inadvertently resulted from this explosion of affordable PC technology was an office in which every single department (and ultimately every employee) had its *own* PC. On that PC were programs to help that one department or worker do her job better, the transactional systems we discussed above—and at most arts organizations, not much has changed in 30 years, in this respect.

How CRM Solves This Problem

Customer Relationship Management systems offer an entirely different approach to office operations. What makes a CRM system so radically different is that it is fundamentally not a transactional system. Rather, a CRM system starts with a different goal: It puts the customer at the center by integrating the functions of all departments into one aggregated database and management tool.

CRM systems provide office workers and managers across departments with a single place to capture and store all of their interactions with a patron. With customer and prospect information collected in this manner, managers can report on it, act on it, and continually update it. Each and every e-mail campaign, ticket purchase, donation, or any other kind of interaction with a particular patron (including individual e-mail correspondence and documented phone calls) exists as a single database entry, all associated with the patron's record. The history of that patron's relationship with your organization is evident in the accumulation of all of those data entries over time.

For instance, Shannon Manning's record in the Laboratory Theatre's CRM system might look like this:

Shannon Manning

350 Baltic St (914)374-9311
Brooklyn, NY 11201 shannon@pt.com

$100 Donation	9/1/09	Annual Fund
$50 Donation	7/13/08	Annual Fund
$200 Donation	10/14/07	Annual Fund
$40 In-Kind Donation	6/15/07	Bingo Night
$150 Donation	12/1/06	Annual Fund
Savion Glover	11/11/08	2 Tickets
Romeo & Juliet	6/14/08	4 Tickets
In the Heights	3/22/08	1 Ticket
Dinosaurs Alive	3/19/08	2 Tickets
E-mail: thank you!	8/31/09	Jane Smith
E-mail: volunteering?	7/31/09	Jane Smith
Donation Acknowledgment	7/15/09	John Fundraiser
E-mail newsletter	9/12/09	Opened 9/12
E-mail postcard	9/3/09	Unopened
E-mail postcard	8/22/09	Opened 8/23

$$$

The vast majority of this data is collected automatically. For example, when Shannon buys a ticket online, that transaction is instantly captured in the CRM system. When a staff member sends Shannon an e-mail, it too is automatically added to her record. Other pieces of information are entered manually; for example, when a staff member has a phone call with Shannon, he can take notes and store them as a record connected with her account.

The important thing is that each of these elements becomes a discrete, reportable object in the database. As a consequence, the entire history of Shannon's relationship with your organization is evident in the accumulation of all of these objects over time.

Right now, if organizations even have a place to store these bits of information digitally, they typically save them in a "notes" field in a ticketing or donor database that looks something like this:

> June - Sept: 3 shows. Outdoor theatre in city park 10/22-sending. SS 5/3-LM. CM 5/19-LM. CM 5/25-LM. CM 5/31-LM. CM 5/31-Board member called and said Bill is no longer attending. Put her on the mailing list and send the schedule. CM 6/1-RI thru 8/00. BZ

This might as well be written in code! In this case, the information is, for all intents and purposes, lost. You can't search for it or access the data for a report or even use it to classify your patrons. In a CRM system, on the other hand, all data is structured and searchable.

A Day in the Life of an Organization Using CRM

Let's look in a little more detail at how patron data would be handled, to see exactly how a CRM system will help you run your organization differently, and better.

Let's say the same Shannon Manning calls the office with a question about an upcoming event and speaks to Jane. When the call is over, Jane accesses Shannon's record in the CRM system from her computer.

Jane creates a new "activity" entry and types in a summary of the phone call:

> Shannon called to talk about the Spring Gala—she wants to know if she can reserve a few extra seats for friends who are potential donors. I told her that should be fine, and that I would check in with her as the event approaches.

During the call Jane had promised to call Shannon back in a month, and agreed to have the box office put Shannon's upcoming tickets in the mail. So, in addition to the summary above, Jane creates a follow-up task for herself. Because this task is in the CRM system, it will show up on her calendar in a month with a reminder, and will be visible to anyone else in the company who may have contact with Shannon in the meantime. She also enters another task and assigns it to Joe in the box office, asking him to take care of mailing Shannon's tickets out. That task will show up on Joe's to-do list immediately.

Then, a month later, the follow-up task shows up automatically on Jane's calendar. At that point, she clicks on Shannon's record and reviews the history of the conversation she had a month before, and gets back in touch with Shannon. Unlike her previous method of keeping such tasks in a stand-alone to-do list, Jane doesn't have deal with deciphering a coded "notes" field in a separate fundraising or ticketing system to remind herself of what happened. She can see the time-stamped record of the phone call in the context of all of Jane's other activities with the organization.

The key to embracing CRM, and the central benefit to an organization using it, is that every contact and every transaction with every patron is documented in one central location. In this way, CRM represents a fundamental change in the way an organization is run, and when everyone participates, the result is a dramatic improvement the way the organization connects with its patrons.

Chapter 13

Five CRM Wall Breakers

Earlier, we promised that CRM would offer revolutionary change. In theory, it's easy to see the technological improvements CRM represents. But what does it really mean for your organization?

Below we list five business objectives that CRM enables your organization to achieve quickly and easily. As you read these, ask yourself how much better off your organization would be if you could achieve all of these objectives, and continue to do so on an ongoing basis.

1. Reduce churn and build patron loyalty

A study conducted in 2008 by the international consulting firm Oliver Wymann for a group of nine major symphony orchestra marketing directors revealed that the vast majority of customers who attend a performance for the first time do not return. Specifically, 90 percent of first-time concertgoers don't purchase tickets for a second concert in the following season.

The sad truth is that this experience is endemic to the arts world. The arts are an industry in which organizations work hard raising money to spend on marketing, print, direct mail, and telemarketing, and often achieve initial success in finding new patrons to build up the "the audience of the future."

The shame is that once they are successful in bringing in these new people, most organizations see this "audience of the future" only once. There is a revolving door of new patrons in and out, and then the process begins all over again the next year.

But what if you could dramatically reduce that churn and improve the proportion of people who come back even once or twice more? Wouldn't the balance of your economic fortune shift dramatically? The only way to do that is by building long-term customer relationships and engaging with patrons in a meaningful way.

Here's a short case history to show how this process might look.

Jack McAuliffe, a consultant in the symphony world, is currently working with several orchestras to implement a churn-reducing strategy. At his suggestion, they send e-mail to all first-time patrons a day or two after they have attended their first performance, inviting the attendees to take a short survey about their recent experience. In return they receive a special ticket offer from the orchestra.

Normally, based on industry-average open rates, one might expect 20 to 25 percent of the recipients to open the e-mail. However, Jack found on average that 40 to 50 percent not only opened the e-mail, but actually took the survey. That's already an astounding success rate.

From the surveys, the orchestras began to see what motivated first-time concertgoers, the demographic makeup of this audience, and how these new customers first heard about the concert. If the orchestras posed the right questions well, they ended up with good qualitative survey data to work with.

But information was not the orchestras' real purpose in sending out the surveys. The real motivation for sending the survey was to turn first-time patrons into repeat audience members. The very act of taking the survey gave customers the opportunity to revisit their experience, which reinforced its effect on them. For example, a question about what part of the concert she enjoyed most encouraged the patron to articulate her positive experience, thus establishing it more firmly in her mind.

This subtle nurturing of the patron continued as the respondent clicked "done" at the end of the survey and received an immediate "thank you" discount offer for another performance.

Of the 40 to 50 percent of first-time attendees who took the survey for each organization, between 15 and 30 percent purchased another ticket! In other words, *this approach encouraged up to 30 percent of first-time attendees to return for a second performance of the orchestra.* And customers who attend two or more performances in one season are up to ten times more likely to subscribe the next season than those who attend only once.

Talk about reducing churn!

So how does a CRM system help you do this?

In order to implement this kind of strategy, you need to be able to quickly and easily run a report of all ticket buyers for the previous night's concert, figure out which ones are *first-time* buyers, and then send out an e-mail to them right away. With a CRM system, reaching out to first-time patrons within 48 hours of an event doesn't even require a coordinated effort across departments—one person can handle the whole process in a few clicks, or even on an automated basis. Not only does the data exist, it's all accessible in one place.

2. Solicit every donor as you would a major donor

In most arts organizations, the development department should be employing many of the same Fifth Wall-breaking practices we are advocating for arts marketers.

And they usually already do, and do it well. But only to a very narrow segment of the patrons. Think about it. Your major donors continue to give you money because you know them and treat them as special patrons. You communicate with them in a personalized way. You solicit donations from them knowing their giving history, as well as their giving potential. Your asks are targeted and meaningful.

But most organizations don't treat *every* donor like a major donor. Instead, they conduct mass fundraising campaigns, sending the same appeal to nearly everyone on the mailing list, beyond the top tier. Anyone who has been involved in this sort of fundraising knows exactly how disappointing the results typically are.

A personalized approach is simply more effective. Last year when we first started writing this book, Gene made an end-of-year donation of several hundred dollars to an organization whose events he had attended frequently that past summer. It was the first time he had donated to this organization, and it was a relatively large donation, given his overall budget for philanthropic giving.

It was more than a month before Gene heard from the organization. When he finally did, it was a form letter and a printed acknowledgment thanking him for joining. That's it, nothing personal, not even an acknowledgment that he was a first-time donor. He was, however, added to an e-mail newsletter for donors. Because he didn't opt in to receive it, at first he thought it was spam.

Gene got a few e-mails during the summer while events were going on. Nothing was personalized. But a year after making that first donation, he got an e-mail asking him to renew his gift. Needless to say, he was lukewarm on the renewal. Why? Because he didn't feel connected to the organization in any meaningful way.

What a huge missed opportunity! Do you blame him for feeling somewhat rejected by that organization, even a bit slighted? We don't think that's how any organization would want a first-time donor to feel.

CRM systems enable you to change this. With CRM, you can quickly and easily send more personalized acknowledgment letters, because you always have a donor's complete history right at your fingertips. What if this organization had recognized Gene's first-time donation, and then spent the season keeping an eye on his attendance and tracking whether he ever opened or clicked on their "donor-only" e-mails?

Then, when it came time to renew, they could tailor their ask based on his actual interactions with the organization, with a personalized e-mail or letter that said, "Thank you for last year's gift of $XX. We hope you enjoyed [x y z performances] and our e-mails, and we hope that you'll consider renewing your gift this year." If Gene had received *that* letter, and felt as if he were treated as an individual rather than one of thousands of other nameless donors, he'd be more likely to renew.

A development director will probably be able to rattle off the top of his head not only the names of his organization's top ten donors but also details about their lives: spouse's name, number of kids, where the daughter is attending college, etc. A CRM system enables him, and the rest of the department, to *pretend* to 100 percent of their donors that they remember all of that information. Even smaller or less frequent donors can feel appreciated, as if they have a personal connection to the organization.

3. Perform only segmented marketing and fundraising

Earlier, we discussed the importance of targeted marketing when using e-mail. Too often, arts organizations click "send to all" in their e-mail campaigns, or send the very same direct-mail piece to every person on their mailing list. This practice violates the cardinal rule of direct marketing in so many ways it's a wonder that arts organizations get even a .5-percent response rate. Tons of evidence suggest that *targeted* e-mail and *targeted* direct-mail marketing are a far better use of resources than mass marketing.

Plenty of books cover the fundamentals of direct-mail marketing and fundraising, so we won't repeat them here. But at least one basic principle deserves a place in our discussion: Savvy marketers know that a great response rate comes more from the *quality* of your list than the form of the solicitation itself. Good lists get good response rates. Great lists get great response rates.

A rich database in a CRM system will enable you to hone your list and dramatically improve your results. If you can classify your ticket buyers by frequency, zip code, type of performance they prefer, or how much money they've given, and target your marketing message accordingly, you'll see better results.

You can even customize solicitations on a much finer level, sending one message to frequent donors, another to donors who gave money last year but not this year, and another to patrons who buy tickets but have never donated at all. Once you have access to the sophisticated reporting capabilities of a CRM system, you can target your fundraising appeals in a much more intelligent way.

When you can tailor fundraising and marketing efforts based on giving and attendance history, when you can personalize a message, and make appeals in a professional manner, good results will follow. Here's one example:

> Charlie Wade, Vice President for Marketing at the Atlanta Symphony, reports that after a series of internal meetings between the marketing and development staffs it was agreed that the responsibility for soliciting donors who give $1,749 or less was better suited to the marketing department.

> In the past, the orchestra had approached their patrons without sufficient regard to the number of multiple fundraising and subscription sales pitches that patrons were receiving as each department worked to meet their individual fundraising and sales goals.

> The new alignment between the two departments led to the beginning of a long term—more cooperative—strategy for an improved patron experience. "We think we have stopped the bleeding," said Wade. "For instance, the rate of patrons asking to

be placed on the 'Do Not Call' list has fallen by almost 50 percent." And regular meetings are held with box office, marketing, and development staff to specifically focus on the patron experience.

Equally important, says Wade, is applying the basics of market segmentation to mass fundraising versus one message for all. "I'm sure that other non-profits are way ahead of the curve on this, but my sense is that arts organizations almost universally send out the same message to all their low-end donors. We are trying, with the help of market research, to segment our messaging based on what we think a particular portion of our audience will respond to.

"It was a bit of an 'aha' when we realized that a $50 or $100 contribution was essentially the result of a marketing campaign and not a traditional high-end development strategy. That allowed us to see that we needed to match up our skill sets to fit the various patron groups," continued Wade. "We essentially segmented *ourselves* to better serve our patrons." The result in the first year was a net improvement of more than $100,000 to the Orchestra's bottom line, which was achieved primarily through cost control and more concentrated campaigns. "While we actually had slightly fewer donors since we stopped year-round soliciting, we significantly reduced the spend rate on every dollar raised by about 33 percent," said Wade.

What this experience makes clear is that marketing and fundraising are really members of the same family. The segmentation and messaging techniques carefully honed in marketing departments are completely transferable to philanthropy. And when they are, better results will be realized.

Recently, Gene was at a meeting with a senior executive from American Express, someone whose job happens to be developing marketing partnerships with arts and entertainment organizations. They started talking about some of the leading arts organizations in New York City, and she said, referring to one of the most prestigious ones, "Can you please tell them to stop calling me at home all the time? One week I'll get a telemarketing call, followed by a solicitation from the development department, followed by a direct-mail piece, and then another phone call from the subscriptions department. They are driving me crazy."

With CRM, targeted marketing is the norm. If you focus simply on communicating with your patrons in a personalized way, providing them with great customer service, and not accidentally telemarketing to them three times in the same week, you'll be sending them a very clear signal that they matter to you. This is an important part of breaking the Fifth Wall.

4. Improve staff efficiency and collaboration

When you have transactional systems, each staff member is working in his own private universe. Each person documents phone calls, processes ticket sales, and schedules meetings in his own manner, using his own methods. It's very hard to develop a sense of teamwork and shared purpose in a company that operates like this.

Now imagine that every employee, from the executive director to the newest member of your customer-service staff, works off of a shared system. Imagine that your box-office manager has an interaction with a patron and realizes she's a major donor. He needs the executive director to be aware of it, so with a single click he could document that call and send a message to the executive director.

Imagine how much more productive your staff could be if your office technology could enable them to work in a collaborative way each and every day. CRM provides this common platform. It increases the efficiency of your staff, fosters teamwork, and eliminates missed opportunities so things don't fall into black holes.

This kind of cooperation and cohesion—"staff alignment"—is nearly unheard of in the arts today, yet it's increasingly commonplace in the corporate use of CRM.

From the very first day of adopting CRM, each staff member logs on and starts using a common system, and a new level of teamwork happens instantly. Imagine that a patron calls the box office to say that their parking passes (that came along with their donation) had been lost. The box-office manager documents the call, and assigns a "task" for the development department to send out a new parking pass. The development department handles the request, and documents it. Now, three weeks later, when the patron calls or e-mails the box office, the box-office manager says, "I see we sent you a new parking pass. Did you get it?"

This may seem trivial, but as you saw before, this notion of connectedness is becoming paramount in our very fragmented world. When that patron calls your organization, she just wants her problem solved by whomever it is that answers the phone—she doesn't care that parking passes aren't handled by the box office. Staff alignment means better customer service, which, when added to the quality of the cultural events you produce, will make that patron a more loyal participant and/or donor.

5. Eliminate institutional memory loss

If for no other reason, CRM will revolutionize the arts because it eliminates institutional memory loss. When a key member of your staff, your development director, for example, leaves the organization, she takes with her all the conversations she's had with your key donors and board members. Sure, she's kept copies of letters in paper files and maybe Microsoft Word documents somewhere on her PC. But imagine what it will take to find and organize all that information.

We are constantly astounded by the amount of valuable personal information that is stored in staff members' heads. Most development departments do have a personal relationship with many of their donors, but that relationship is confined to the particular person in the job. Their individual interactions—lunches, parties, e-mails, and phone calls—exist only as long as that staff member continues to work for your organization. When she moves on, that history is gone.

Instead, imagine if all those interactions were documented in a way that's easily accessible to everyone on your staff. Every phone call, lunch meeting, and fundraising event is documented in one place. This way, if there is staff turnover, it doesn't mean starting from scratch; you can have continuity in your operation, and the person coming into the job can more quickly pick up where their predecessor left off.

Using a CRM system, your staff is writing the history of your organization every day. They are creating an integrated record of your relationship with your patrons, and it's being stored permanently and in a retrievable, organized way.

The benchmark of success for any arts organization lies in its ability to establish continuing relationships with its patrons. To attain that goal, the documentation of those relationships is a key asset of the organization. Most organizations don't even have this asset—and if they do, they probably have no idea where all the scattered records are hiding in their office.

Institutional memory loss is one of non-profits' biggest problems, and CRM eliminates it from day one.

CRM Addresses Today's Needs Head On

If you could accomplish all these goals (reducing churn, cultivating all your donors, segmenting your marketing efforts, aligning your staff, and solving institutional memory loss), ask yourself: How much better off would your organization be?

Maybe you have already solved one or even two of these issues. Our guess is that you'd agree that current office technology, or at least, the way we currently use our technological resources, doesn't give you the necessary tools to attain these benchmarks effectively or easily.

But our bet is that you can accomplish *all* of these goals by adopting a CRM system, which is now available for the arts. By now you're probably wondering how CRM could possibly be affordable for non-profit arts organizations if it's a technology driving corporate America. It's affordable because the basic infrastructure of many CRM systems—cloud computing—is completely scalable to the size of the organization.

In the next chapter we'll take a look at how cloud computing works.

Chapter 14

Cloud Computing

To set the stage, let's look at how technology for the arts industry is offered and priced today.

Here's a perceptual map showing software systems for the arts, with price and features as the main variables.

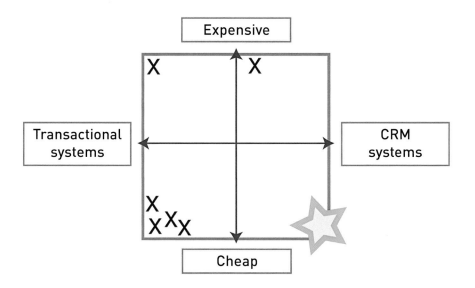

As you can see on the chart, down in the left corner we have a plethora of inexpensive transactional systems, such as donor databases, ticketing systems, and e-mail marketing programs.

The top left quadrant represents expensive alternatives that are more robust and complex but are still ultimately single-purpose transactional systems that enable larger organizations to manage their donor relations.

A little bit further to the right across the top, also on the expensive end of the spectrum, are systems that combine ticketing and donations. In the 1990s, the notion of combining ticketing and fundraising was itself a revolutionary idea and systems that accomplish this are, in a sense, precursors to the full-featured CRM systems available today.

But those systems are costly—not only is there generally a big upfront licensing fee, but operating them requires technology administrators and in-house servers, all at additional cost.

The goal, of course, would be to find a system that fits into the very bottom right corner—a single CRM system that all departments can use to manage their data and day-to-day tasks, *and* that fits into the budget of even small non-profit organizations. That goal is now possible, and the reason is cloud computing. When you combine CRM systems with cloud computing and open platforms, you get a powerhouse of technology capability that has never been seen before in business, or in the arts industry.

To explain what cloud computing is, let's first look at how we got here.

The History of CRM

CRM itself is neither a new concept nor a new technology. Arts consultant Steven Roth teaches a course about it at the Boston University Graduate School of Management and was involved in the early days of CRM. He provides this history of CRM in the business world:

> The term Customer Relationship Management (CRM) began to appear in the mid-to-late 1990s. Industries such as financial services, telecommunications, and retail were early adopters. These industries had the following characteristics in common:

business-to-consumer marketing, a large number of customers, high interaction frequency with customers, direct access to customers, and large data repositories.[12]

CRM was touted as the "next big thing" but no one really understood what it meant. CRM implementation was difficult, time-consuming, and very costly. Implementations could take years, and expectations were sky high. CRM became a classic case of over-promising and under-delivering, and the concept fell out of favor in the early 2000s.

CRM began to emerge from exile in the mid-2000s. Reduced costs of data management and storage, more reasonable expectations, and more targeted implementations—along with the emergence of the Internet as a mainstream business tool—brought CRM back into vogue. In addition, the field of marketing was changing to a more analytical, measurement-based discipline.

Companies of all sizes began to see the value of CRM as an over-arching business strategy instead of a quick-fix technology. Flexible CRM providers have helped bring us to current times where CRM is accessible to companies of all sizes in the commercial and non-profit sectors.

Today, hundreds of thousands of corporations use CRM systems. One of the industry-leading CRM providers, salesforce.com, a Silicon Valley company formed about a decade ago, has already amassed 80,000 corporate customers. And it is only one of many companies in the CRM industry. The corporate world has figured out that CRM is the way to run their businesses!

Salesforce.com has led the way in providing CRM at an affordable price by moving its technology to the "cloud." If you've read any technology-related article recently, you've likely seen the phrase "cloud computing." Cloud computing is fundamentally a new method by which technology is made available or delivered.

Remember the mainframe computers we discussed in Chapter 12. Back in the 1960s, they were costly, giant refrigerator-like machines in the basement of large buildings, run by professional database administrators.

Then in the 1980s, the PC arrived and computing power was available on the desktop. You would sometimes access a shared server for certain programs or data. These servers were still running somewhere on-site, incurring power and maintenance costs and requiring a system administrator to keep them running smoothly.

Today, though, there's another option. Servers have moved off-site. Giant "server farms" have sprouted up in highly protected, bunker-like buildings, where hundreds, if not thousands, of networked computers operate with dramatic efficiency, run by relatively few staff members. Access to those computers is not by wires running to the basement. It's wireless, over the Internet.

In a nutshell, this is the technology architecture known as cloud computing. Those big servers out there online are "in the cloud"—you never visit them, and there's no physical connection, but you always know that they're there. The current Wikipedia definition of cloud computing is: "Internet-based computing, whereby shared resources, software and information are provided to computers and other devices *on-demand*, like a traditional utility."

We are all familiar with this concept of *on-demand* access, but perhaps we take it for granted. You probably don't power your home by buying and owning your own generator in your backyard. Rather, you lease power from a utility company and pay only for what you use. Cloud computing works with the same idea: Lease server power and space on demand, and pay only for what you use. Because you pay based upon usage, the system is eminently scalable. If you are a big organization, you use more and pay more; the reverse goes for small organizations. Cloud computing, then, is suitable for everyone, both big businesses and small non-profits.

Here's an example close to home: Our company, Patron Technology, doesn't own or lease servers anymore. We operate entirely in the cloud.

That means we don't worry about a server we own failing, and we never have to call anyone to replace a hard drive. Our PatronMail servers are hosted in a state-of-the-art cloud-computing center in Texas, which we have never seen or visited.

In this model, your organization's data resides in one place, and is accessible to everyone in the organization, whether they are at a remote box office, working at home, in different departments, or on a different floor. Indeed, we have PatronManager CRM clients that are such small theatre companies that they don't even have an office. No matter: They can operate as if they do, because they are using a CRM system in the cloud.

Cloud computing is a distinctly different and less expensive way to deliver software. And while lower price is a key benefit, there are many others:

> **No servers means fast setup.** Again, in a cloud-computing environment, you don't need to own or manage any servers. Your IT staff (if you have one) will be happy because they won't have to work as hard to manage your technology infrastructure. With cloud computing, you are leasing someone else's technology, and they provide much of the support for it. Because cloud computing is Internet-based, it is by nature "plug and play." That means setup is often wizard-driven and relatively quick. There's no waiting for servers to show up and be installed, and no time is spent formatting hard drives.

> **Convenience.** You can access your data from any computer browser at any time, as long as you have an Internet connection.

> **Green.** Of course, owning fewer servers is better for our planet. Rather than using tons of energy and natural resources to mold plastic and silicon and metal into dozens of computers, we can share a larger server with hundreds or even thousands of other companies.

Security. When we talk to arts organizations about cloud computing, their immediate reaction is to ask, "But wait, how secure is my data?" First of all, world-class corporations like FedEx, JP Morgan, and Dell Computers all rely on data storage in the cloud—CRM providers like salesforce.com have multiple layers of redundancy in their data backups.

That said, trusting your data in a cloud environment does carry some element of risk. But that risk is far less than the risk of maintaining your own data security and backup systems without state-of-the-art hardware. And, for an added measure of data security, there's an easy way to lower your risk to almost nothing: Download your data weekly (or daily) from the cloud to your office PC as a backup. This way, your data end up being much more secure than they were before cloud computing.

Now that you've read more about CRM and cloud computing, we hope you understand why the big fat claim at the beginning of this section has merit. Running your organization with CRM will not simply replace current systems with better ones. It will fundamentally change the way you run your business.

A CRM system will enable you to do better e-mail marketing by segmenting your patrons better. It will allow you to do smarter fundraising because the inherent reporting capabilities in CRM will personalize and streamline your fundraising operations. It will allow your staff to work as a team in a way that they never have before, whether working in your office, or at home. And ultimately, it will allow you to optimize your marketing spend and sell more tickets.

As we said at the start, while CRM systems are technology driven, they are at the same time a new managerial framework into which you can sort your organization's daily activities. Now may be the first time since the introduction of the computer into arts management that such a truly radical change has come to the arts industry.

We are evangelists for CRM because we've seen how it has completely transformed our own business. In 2001 we adopted the web-based

CRM system offered by salesforce.com. Back then, it was brand new, rudimentary, and much less robust than it is today. But as the years went on, our company embraced CRM, and as a result, ten years later, we now have a master database in which our staff has documented every single phone call, every e-mail, every meeting, and every contract with each and every one of our customers and potential customers.

It's frequently the case that we get a call from a new marketing director at a client organization who says that she was left no documentation by her predecessor, and asks that we update her on where we stand in our business relationship. We simply cut and paste the last six months of correspondence with her predecessor and bring her up to speed with very little effort.

It is hard for us to conceive of running our business in any other way today. CRM has made our organization more efficient, and therefore our co-workers are more productive. We spend almost no time "spinning our wheels" looking for data or reports, and more time doing essential work.

If we were to turn the clock back and remove CRM from our daily operations, we could certainly still have a functional operation. But we would take a huge hit in productivity. Though it can't be easily measured, a quick survey of our staff suggests most frequent data-related tasks would take us at least 25 percent longer to do. In the end, CRM is all about running our organization in the smartest and most efficient way possible.

In an era in which raising money is increasingly difficult and the revenue side of the ledger is squeezed, being more efficient with your staff time is tantamount to raising more money. If you can find a way to get 25 percent more work accomplished by the same staff, how much more successful would your organization be?

We are completely committed to CRM because it has revolutionized the way we operate, and we have no doubt that CRM will do the same for the arts industry.

SECTION VI: Conclusion

Chapter 15

Beyond the Fifth Wall: Predictions for the Future

At the beginning of this book, we considered how the marketing world of arts managers has changed dramatically over the past decade. And judging from the plethora of new portable Internet devices coming on the market, the speed at which sites like Facebook and Google are innovating, and continued miniaturization of computing devices, there is every reason to believe that this same rate of change will continue.

Many of the dramatic improvements in the consumer web experience have been driven by increases in bandwidth. In the mid-1990s when Internet access was limited to dial-up, sites with text and pictures were the norm. Then as broadband, DSL, and cable became common, streaming audio and video emerged and YouTube changed the web forever. We're now on the doorstep of yet another big change, with the introduction of 4G wireless networks, which will make the Internet connection on your mobile device as fast as your home broadband connection.

Arts marketers ought to pay a good deal of attention to the emerging trends in the world of technology. Most every commercial industry is embracing technology more quickly than ever before and trying to innovate to improve their businesses, and indeed there are some notable examples in our field. Damian Bazadona has created Situation Interactive, a highly regarded and intensely creative media company that manages the online marketing strategy for over 200 live-event productions and currently represents many theatrical productions across the country including *Wicked*, *Mamma Mia!*, *Billy Elliot*, and *Blue Man Group*. His company, working with the Broadway production of *Hair*, managed to get permission from the unions to tape the dance party that happened at the end of each show, and post it on Facebook for audience members to find and tag themselves.

Our field is filled with lots of other creative, industrious, and innovative people. Technology costs a lot less to develop than it did only a decade ago, and the opportunities are limited more by imagination than anything else. So, let's put our culture of creativity and innovation to work in the arts! There's no reason why the arts shouldn't be a leader in terms of exploiting new technology.

Gene's three previous books each concluded with predictions for the future. Looking back on these, many of them turned out to be right on target. In 2004 he wrote about the "ASP (Application Service Provider) model" of software, which would allow an organization to someday abandon their separate, unsynchronized PC software systems and have data that "finally ends up in one place." The acronym has changed, but CRM and cloud computing have realized that dream. And in 2005 he suggested that in the near future, "in all likelihood, [patrons] will be checking their mobile computing devices as compulsively as they use their cell phones today!"

So in keeping with tradition, Gene is taking the lead on this chapter to offer predictions about some of the most interesting and relevant technology trends that arts managers ought to be aware of. As with any predictions, it's likely that some of these ideas won't reach their full potential, but each is worth contemplating in terms of how it could improve your ability to break the Fifth Wall.

1. Mobile technology and the ubiquitous web

The iPhone and other smartphones bear little resemblance to the first cell phones. We need to think of them as small computers, with phones, cameras, music players, and Internet browsing all built in. Because of rapid advances in technology, more and more computing power can be placed in ever-smaller devices.

In the future, it's safe to expect even further collapsing of the boundaries separating desktop computers, laptops, and portable smartphones. The iPhone has already spawned the iPad, and there will be copycats and further iterations. As wireless devices become cheaper, more and more people will have them—and that means that soon enough, most people will connect to the web wherever they are, whenever they want. The notion of checking e-mail "when you get home" will go the way of the rotary telephone.

For years, the notion of community-wide Internet access has been discussed by city and county governments. Google once promised to offer Wi-Fi service for all of Silicon Valley; other, similar initiatives were also announced. To date, some neighborhood access zones have materialized, but nothing on the grand scale once envisioned. Nevertheless, Internet access is becoming cheaper, easier, and ubiquitous. Recently, Starbucks began offering free Wi-Fi in its cafes, and most corporate hotel chains for business travelers (such as Hilton Garden Inn) offer free Wi-Fi as well. Even airlines are beginning to offer inflight Wi-Fi. It will take some time, but soon enough, retailers will recognize that free Wi-Fi draws people to their locations. Should your lobby offer it too?

Think about the implications of widespread, mobile Internet access. Your ability to reach patrons throughout their day not just with relevant content but also relevant purchase opportunities (such as a performance discount for that night) is becoming easier. If you've broken the Fifth Wall and have built a meaningful digital connection with your patrons, they will pay attention to your messages and respond more rapidly than they are doing today.

Let's take the trend of last-minute ticket buying to its logical extreme. Imagine Shannon and Albert Manning are sitting at a café right around the corner from your venue. An e-mail arrives on Shannon's smartphone saying, "Curtain goes up in 35 minutes for *Pal Joey*. Great seats are still available—click here."

2. Pervasive live streaming & microbroadcasting

Live streaming media—the notion of *real-time* web broadcasting—is going to become commonplace. Companies such as ustream.tv, qik. com, and justin.tv are jockeying for a leadership position, and may very well become household names in the near future.

On a chilly evening last summer, I was at an outdoor concert at Tanglewood, sitting in the very back. The Boston Symphony had recently installed high-definition TV screens in the rear of the 6,000-seat Koussevitzky Music Shed where it performs. In the past, those seats were so far away that you could barely see the stage. Suddenly, the experience is entirely different. You hear the music live while watching close-ups of the musicians as if you're at home in your living room. The camera direction is terrific and completely professional. I had thought video would violate the well-worn experience of concertgoing, but instead it was new and enjoyable way to experience a concert.

The point is: If the Boston Symphony has already invested in video cameras, directors, and staff to make these in-venue broadcasts possible, it's not a stretch to imagine that they will eventually stream them live online. In time, the Boston Symphony and others will recognize the same thing that major sports teams already understand: When you broadcast, you don't cannibalize your audience. Rather, you entice them to come to see the event live. (That's certainly what the live Met Opera is proving with its high-definition movie-theatre broadcasts today.)

The technology to broadcast live video streams is almost cheap enough that virtually *every arts organization could become a potential broadcaster*. I'll bet that common sense will prevail among unions and arts organizations and they will find a way to enable live broadcasting more openly. If they don't, others will jump in. My alma mater, Oberlin College and Conservatory, has already made plans to broadcast every Oberlin Orchestra concert and student recital. In Europe, the Berlin Philharmonic is doing it right now, and classicaltv.com and medici. tv stream live and recorded classical-music concerts from all over the European continent.

For other arts genres, live broadcasting may be easier. There are tons of non-union theatres and dance companies that don't have the same regulations to get around. Beyond performances, I can easily imagine live backstage interviews with performers, preconcert talks, and museum lectures all streamed live.

The future of arts broadcasting lies in the hands of individual arts organizations, which will find that creating their own broadcasts will be a new and powerful way to break the Fifth Wall. They will be able to provide riveting programming that has never before been available, stirring interest and motivating patrons to attend their live events.

3. Geolocation

Another technological innovation about to go mainstream is geolocation. Quite simply, geolocation technology embedded within a smartphone or other mobile device will enable you to find relevant and timely information based on where you are at a given moment. The same technology also enables you to broadcast your whereabouts, should you choose to. I experienced this technology some weeks ago when I was in the West Village looking for one of my favorite restaurants, which had, much to my dismay, closed down. A friend with me simply checked her iPhone, which showed us about twenty restaurants (and relevant reviews) within two blocks of where we were standing.

Location-based social platforms like Foursquare, Facebook Places, Loopt, and Gowalla are gaining a lot of traction today. The reach of most of these services is still small, but their existence foretells the future.

The idea behind these services is that you sign up for an account and download an app to your geolocation-enabled smartphone. Then when you're out on the town—whether "on the town" means bar-hopping on a Saturday night or just going to dinner and the theatre with friends, or going away on a business trip—you take a moment to "check in" at each location when you arrive by opening the app on your phone, letting the geolocation technology figure out where you are, and then touching the "check in" button for the restaurant, theatre, or hotel. Your friends who also use the app can see that you've checked in—and you can see who else is currently at the bar with you! People can also leave "tips" for other users, like, "Heather the barista makes the best frappuccinos" or, "don't order the sweet-potato fries." Can you imagine the implications for audience members who check in to your venues, and discover their friends are at the same performance?

The technology gets interesting for marketers because businesses can offer specials and discounts on these platforms. For example, a bar might offer a special on Foursquare where if you check in at the bar three times in a month, you can get a free glass of wine. You'll see that this deal is available when you go to check in at the bar, but even more importantly, you'll see it if you check in *somewhere else nearby*—say, a restaurant down the street from that bar. The app will tell you if there's a deal available in your vicinity, not just at the location where you currently are.

Imagine how useful this could be for the arts. It's not a stretch to imagine someone sitting at a restaurant at 6:30 in the evening, checking in to one of these apps, and noticing that the theatre across the street is offering discounted tickets for anyone who comes and checks in there! That theatre is taking advantage of an opportunity to break the Fifth Wall in an almost-literal way, reaching out just beyond its venue walls and drawing patrons in.

4. Stored-Value Tickets

The physical ticket, a piece of paper that represents the fact that you have paid for entrance to an event, is an outdated technology. A ticket can be much more than that. Imagine a ticket that works like a stored-value debit card, enabling you add value to it and then buy things at the venue without cash or another payment method. Why don't we sell prepaid parking, CDs, or even wine and snacks *when we're selling a ticket*? Make it easier for patrons to buy more from you by letting them buy it up front.

It always enrages me when I get to intermission at a big hall and there's a single bartender pouring drinks and collecting money. The short twenty-minute break is taken up by a stressful ten-minute wait standing in line, leaving just enough time to gulp down a glass of wine. How much more enjoyable would it be if the payment portion of that transaction were eliminated by prepurchasing the drinks? This is done in Europe as standard practice. In most theatres in London, your drinks can be waiting for you at intermission, paid for well in advance, and there are already beginning to be venues in New York and other cities that offer this.

Eventually, some sort of smart-card technology (or perhaps a feature on your smartphone) will dominate and perhaps replace the traditional ticket. Smart tickets will open new avenues for better customer service and creative pricing options, and will improve the arts-going experience for patrons at the same time.

5. Open Platforms

Perhaps the best way to talk about open platforms is to use an example that everyone knows about, the Apple iPhone. While the iPhone itself is impressive, the most valuable aspect of it is the ability for users of the iPhone to instantly download "apps" (short for applications) that can customize and extend the utility of the phone itself. These apps expand the traditional notion of what a phone is, by offering everything from games and travel directions to cartoons for children. Today there are over 200,000 apps in the iPhone app store!

Apple correctly realized that if they stayed with a traditional model of software development, by limiting the phone to features that its own programmers developed, it would dramatically restrict the potential utility of the phone, and block out a lot of its potential value. But by inviting the community of programmers and entrepreneurs to develop apps that run on the iPhone, they created a nearly unlimited universe of value for their clients and for their product.

The reason they were able to do this is that the iPhone runs on a "platform." The platform is nothing more than a cloud-based database combined with a series of programming rules that a programmer must follow to publish their app. Once an app is published on the platform, users can instantly download it (for free or a small fee) and begin to use that app. Facebook has done the same thing—there are thousands of Facebook applications built by third-party developers that can be seamlessly loaded into Facebook.

This whole concept of platforms is no less relevant or valuable in the corporate world than it is the consumer world. For example, CRM systems that are built on platforms can be extended in exactly the same way that the iPhone is. Salesforce.com, as of this writing, currently has 85,000 companies and over 2 million users. Its open platform now has over 1,000 business apps that can be instantly installed. This means that Salesforce CRM customers are not limited to the software features that salesforce.com itself creates—they can plug in new business applications as their needs expand.

Gone are the days when arts managers needed to put all their eggs in one technology basket. An open platform allows an ecosystem of programmers all over the world to build software applications that work on that platform. In time, I believe this open-platform world will ultimately replace the old single-source model of the past few decades.

All of these predictions and trends are meant to inspire your creativity. I urge you to take some time to think about them and consider how your organization could leverage them to help you break the Fifth Wall. Don't sit on the sidelines as others experiment. Reserve some time to test new approaches. Arts patrons are becoming accustomed to impressively advanced online technology. Why not become one of the organizations that comes up with the ideas and techniques that will change the future of our field?

Chapter 16

Rethinking Arts Marketing for the 21st Century

A decade ago, in the middle of the dot-com crash, few predicted how quickly the Internet would rebound and forge new and profound changes in how we communicate with each other. In ten short years, the very fundamentals of marketing have been challenged and reshaped.

The corporate world embraced this transformation much more quickly than did the arts. Executives in the corporate world recognized the potential that new technology could afford them, and made huge strides in improving websites, generating paid web traffic, adopting easier-to-use e-commerce technology, and investing time and effort in leveraging social media.

The central question for our industry seems to be whether arts leaders can embrace the changes that are so clearly taking place, and turn their creative and entrepreneurial energies to marketing and audience development with the same energy that they focus on putting art on the stage.

We recognize that arts leaders sometimes struggle with inherently conservative boards, or funders who aren't ready to commit resources to innovation. But if you believe in the version of the arts marketing future we've laid out in this book, then there is simply no choice. It's up to you to help your organization get ahead of the technology curve. As we hope we have proven, there's no reason why the arts industry can't be at the forefront of audience development in the digital age, and indeed, why it can't develop and implement ideas and techniques that the commercial entertainment industry would envy.

At Patron Technology, we work full-time developing new software for a living, and we are looking for partners. We're in this together, and we believe that the traditional divide between vendors and arts organizations is outmoded. Partnership, collaboration, and new business models are the path to a better future.

The biggest challenge is not any of the particular changes themselves, but whether the industry has the will to embrace this "rethinking" we've proposed and go after it. Ours is ultimately a positive message: There is nothing standing in the way of transforming your relationship with your patrons. But you have to first embrace the challenge, and we hope that this book has helped motivate you to do just that, and given you the tools and knowledge to proceed.

We encourage you to make breaking the Fifth Wall the cornerstone of all of your marketing efforts. Start developing closer, interactive relationships with your audience—connect and reconnect digitally and in compelling and creative ways. Use our examples as a starting point, and innovate.

We come to work every day with the goal of helping arts managers blaze a new trail for their industry. By adopting the principles outlined in this book, you can be part of the reinvention of arts marketing for the 21st century.

ENDNOTES

1. Patron Technology Arts Patron Survey, 2006-2010

2. http://www.census.gov/prod/2002pubs/c2kprof00-us.pdf

3. http://www.census.gov/compendia/statab/2010/tables/10s1121.pdf

4. http://pewresearch.org/pubs/1093/generations-online

5. Edison Research Report, April 2010

6. http://www.nickburcher.com/2010/09/facebook-usage-statistics-by-country.html

7. http://www.nytimes.com/2009/10/27/business/media/27audit.html

8. http://www.istrategylabs.com/2010/01/facebook-demographics-and-statistics-report-2010-145-growth-in-1-year/

9. A list of arts organizations mentioned in this chapter:
http://www.facebook.com/pages/Winterthur-Museum-Country-Estate/71681050790
http://www.facebook.com/JerseyArts
http://twitter.com/NatHistoryWhale
http://twitter.com/OperaNinja
http://www.facebook.com/pages/Abingdon-Theatre-Company/65602909885
http://www.facebook.com/AmericanBalletTheatre
http://www.facebook.com/publictheater
http://www.facebook.com/AntaeusTheater
http://www.facebook.com/PilobolusDance
http://twitter.com/TDFNYC

10. For more information: www.newyorklivearts.org

11. http://kcblogger.kennedy-center.org/sites/nso/Lists/Posts/Post.aspx?ID=32

12. *Principles of Customer Relationship Management*, Baran, Galka, and Strunk.

APPENDICES

APPENDIX A

Patron Technology Arts Patron Survey

These are the organizations that participated in the 2010 survey:

92nd Street Y
Atlanta Ballet
Chicago Department of Cultural Affairs
Children's Chorus of Greater Dallas
Choral Arts Ensemble of Rochester
DuPont Theatre
Eugene Symphony
Florentine Opera Company
Florida Stage
Frick Art & Historical Center
Houston Ballet
Music Center - Performing Arts Center of Los Angeles County
Newark Museum
Oakland East Bay Symphony
Oklahoma City Philharmonic
Quick Center for the Arts, Fairfield University
Repertorio Español
San Francisco Performances
Sioux Falls Jazz & Blues Society
Symphony Space
The Morgan Library & Museum
UApresents
The Vilar Performing Arts Center

APPENDIX B

Understanding and Obeying the Anti-Spam Law

The CAN-SPAM (Controlling the Assault of Non-Solicited Pornography and Marketing) Act of 2003 is the first federal law that attempts to regulate what commercial e-mailers can and cannot send. This legislation was updated with four more rules adopted by the Federal Trade Commission in July of 2008, including specific commentary from the FTC clarifying that the Act *does not exempt non-profit organizations* sending commercial e-mail from following its rules.

This is a quick overview to give you an understanding of the law as it stands today. Some of the information presented here is based on conversations with Stephen Cohen, a staff attorney at the Federal Trade Commission and the experiences of LashBack, the e-mail marketing compliance authority and their director of marketing and public affairs, James O'Brien.

Please note that nothing in this chapter is, or is intended to be, legal advice or a legal opinion. It is provided here solely for informational purposes, and since we're dealing with the law, you should also consult with your lawyer. It is also a good idea to seek out an attorney with experience in online marketing regulations.

Enforcing the Law

On December 16, 2003, President Bush signed the CAN-SPAM bill, creating the first federal law regulating commercial e-mail. The objective of this law is to give enforcement power to the FTC to regulate unsolicited e-mail, particularly pornography, and another main focus is to prohibit *deceptive* e-mails, and to give recipients of unwanted e-mail a mechanism for opting out from receiving additional e-mail.

This bill went into effect on January 1, 2004, and since it is the first federal law that addresses e-mail, it supersedes all existing state laws. However, it does not supersede those state laws that are not specific to e-mail, such as trespass, contracts, tort law or any other state law that might relate here. State laws that prohibit falsity or deception in an e-mail still apply, and certain states have been particularly active enforcing their statutes, especially Florida, California, New York, and Washington states. It's no coincidence these are the home states of many of the major technology and advertising companies.

While the CAN-SPAM Act was not designed to restrict legitimate mailers such as arts organizations, it does indeed apply to all organizations, whether for-profit or non-profit.

There have been over 150 CAN-SPAM related prosecutions, and with each one, key aspects of how to comply with this law are becoming clearer. The FTC has recognized the potential for confusion, and actively accepted comments from the business community and others about how to improve the clarity of the law. You can read this dialogue with industry in the Statement of Basis and Purpose, which is published in the Federal Register both for the CAN-SPAM Act and two separate updates or rulemakings that the FTC adopted in 2005 and 2008 respectively.

What kind of e-mail does this apply to?

CAN-SPAM covers commercial e-mail, which is defined as any "electronic mail message whose primary purpose is to sell or promote a product or service." E-mail newsletters that are purely informational, mission-oriented news briefs would not be defined as commercial e-mail. Transactional communications with subscribers such as ticket confirmations or event reminders for tickets that have been purchased are not included either.

However, if your newsletters include articles that refer to events for which you are trying to sell tickets (and they probably do!), then they may fall into the commercial category.

Whether your newsletter is promotional or not depends on what the "primary" purpose of the e-mail message is. In 2005, the FTC clarified "primary purpose" as being defined by the content of the subject line and placement and amount of commercial content in the body of the e-mail. The subject line should not deceive the consumer into opening the e-mail and should be relevant to the content of the message. If you have a commercial offer which takes up 10 percent of your newsletter but is the first thing the consumers see in the preview pane or upon opening, and your subject line features that offer, your newsletter could be perceived as commercial.

As you'll see below, the difference between whether a message is commercial or not will have implications on how you actually write that e-mail and what the subject line is.

Confused yet? Let's see if we can make this a bit clearer!

What the law says:

> **1. Opt-out vs. opt-in:** The CAN-SPAM law is an "opt-out" law. In other words, it obligates you to ensure that anyone who wants to get off your list can do so in a timely manner. However, it doesn't mandate how they get on your list at all. It merely obligates that you compose e-mails to opt-in recipients differently than to those who have not opted in. (In practice, whether you have direct consent to send e-mail or not, we recommend that you follow all requirements for CAN-SPAM compliance.)
>
> Arts organizations are not at all limited in terms of how they collect e-mail names. Although we strongly urge you to get "affirmative consent" (i.e., opt-in sign-ups) from your patrons before mailing to them, getting their permission to do so is not required by this law.

2. Identify your mail as commercial: The law says that if you *don't* have "affirmative consent" from all (or even some) of the patrons on your list, then you must conspicuously label any commercial e-mail message you send to them as an "advertisement or promotion."

What is a commercial message, anyway? Well, as we've seen above, the "primary" purpose of the e-mail is what governs whether it is commercial. However, the law provides no formula or guideline. It would be nice if the law said something like, "If more than 50 percent of your content is commercial, then it's a commercial message." No such luck.

It's really up to you to determine if your message is purely informational or if the primary purpose is to motivate some type of transaction or purchase. For the time being, the best guideline may be those legal cases the FTC has examined already. These cases refer to something called the "net impression" test, which really asks what a reasonable consumer looking at your e-mail would believe its purpose to be.

If you're sending out something that is indeed a commercial message, let's look at what you must do. If you maintain a completely opt-in list (as we recommend), you can send any type of message to that list—including a commercial message—and you have no obligation per the letter of the law to label it in any special way.

However, if you have a mixed list (only some of which are opt-in names) or if you routinely add people who buy tickets through your ticketing system to your list, you are obligated to "clearly and conspicuously" label any commercial e-mail you send them as commercial.

What does clearly and conspicuously mean? Fair question. Does it mean you have to say "This is a commercial e-mail!" in the subject line? Or put it as the first sentence of your e-mail? Or can you bury some language in the footer of the e-mail?

Here's where it gets really murky. Let's focus on the subject line, which is where your patrons decide if your e-mail is worth opening or not.

According to the FTC's Stephen Cohen: "Although the best practice approach suggests that an e-mail subject line should indicate to the recipient that the message is an advertisement or solicitation, neither the law nor the FTC has mandated this yet." Mr. Cohen quickly adds that "Section 5(a) (2) of the Act of course does prohibit deceptive subject lines."

It's up to you, but bear in mind that although the CAN-SPAM Act is silent on this, the FTC Act and/or various state laws regarding unfair or deceptive practices still apply. All you can do is use common sense and consult your own lawyers. If you have any doubts about what you're doing, add the opt-out link and treat the e-mail as commercial.

3. Subject lines must not be confusing: A major requirement of this law is that you not be deceptive with subject lines. In our discussion with the FTC, we looked at the following example:

Let's say you're sending an e-mail about an upcoming *West Side Story* performance and the subject line is "Laboratory Theatre's West Side Story Tickets Still Available." It seems that this subject line is self-evidently referring to a commercial message, so there's probably no need for you to add the words "this is an advertisement" to the subject line.

However, if your subject line is "Laboratory Theatre — News Flash," and your e-mail is all about selling tickets, then that could be seen as deceptive. It certainly wouldn't be obvious by the subject line that this is a commercial message.

In all, it seems that the more clarity you put in your subject line, the safer you will be in terms of keeping within the guidelines of this law, and the better informed your patrons will be.

Again, remember that if you have a 100 percent opt-in list, none of this really applies except for the "no deceptive subject lines" aspect. The requirement of indicating the commercial nature of the e-mail message applies only when you are mailing to patrons who have not opted in. So, using the example above, if you mail your West Side Story ticket announcement with the subject line as merely "Laboratory Theatre — News Flash" to a 100 percent opt-in list, you're completely within the bounds of the law.

4. "Opt-out" requests now have a time limit: The law requires that you remove patrons from your list within ten business days. Our PatronMail system and most other commercial providers offer an instant "one-click" opt-out procedure that immediately removes a patron from your list.

5. Every e-mail must contain a functioning electronic means to opt out: You must provide a way for recipients to opt out online, as opposed to over the phone or by regular mail. Every PatronMail message, and most of those created by other professional e-mail systems, contains a hyperlink at the bottom offering a one-click way for recipients to opt out. This satisfies this provision of the law.

In the rule update, the FTC added that no other information be necessary for a consumer to opt out besides their intent and their e-mail address, and that the unsubscribe process be completed in as close to one click as possible. This means you can't take a consumer through a maze of pages hoping they will get tired and forget unsubscribing. Do not charge a fee to unsubscribe or use confusing language during the process. It is also recommended that you not send an e-mail confirmation when someone unsubscribes.

You can ask why someone is unsubscribing on a web page but you cannot make answering that question a requirement for unsubscribing.

6. Tell them where you are: You must include a valid physical address in every commercial e-mail you send out. The physical address need not be your office address, but it does need to be a "physical" address where you can receive mail, such as a properly registered P.O. Box or street address. This is to ensure that a consumer may write you to opt out of your list. But note that anything that makes you look more transparent, more legitimate, and less like a criminal spammer is going to help not just with compliance, but also with open rates and the overall perception of your brand.

7. Include a privacy policy: It's good business practice to have a clear privacy policy on your website, which states what you will do any information you are collecting about patrons.

Although the CAN-SPAM Act does not require you to have a privacy policy, other federal laws require disclosure and notifying users of how you will use their data.

8. One database for e-mail: If a patron opts out from a marketing e-mail, they should not get e-mail from another department later on. If you do not remove a patron from *all* e-mailings within your organization, you are violating the law.

9. Buying, renting, or swapping lists is okay, but not opt-in: If you buy, rent, or swap lists with any third party and send commercial messages to those lists, then the fact that those lists may be "opt-in" does not release you from the obligation of indicating in the e-mail that your message is a commercial advertisement or promotion.

In other words, a 100 percent opt-in list that has been bought, rented or swapped now must be treated as though it is *not* an opt-in list. You're free to swap lists, but any commercial message you send to a borrowed list must be clearly labeled as described in point 2 above.

The final caveat here is that if you do swap your e-mail list, you must first remove those who have already opted out, and update your list after the swap with anyone who has opted out from the swapped mailing. Just using a borrowed list doesn't give you permission to mail to people who have already opted out of receiving messages from you.

10. Penalties: The law carries a penalty of up to $11,000 per violation. This is serious business. The fines are levied against the "sender," which is likely to be considered the organization, and not the e-mail marketing company or vendor.

The only difference between how for-profit and non-profit companies are treated under this law is in the administration of violations. The FTC generally has no jurisdiction over non-profit organizations, so if a complaint is made against a non-profit, it's likely that that case would be brought by a state attorney general's office for prosecution.

There's a lot of information presented here, but the overall lesson boils down to this: Treat your e-mail subscribers with care and respect. To stand out from the piles of e-mail messages—spam or opt-in—that people receive, it's more important than ever for arts organizations to leverage all of the lessons from Section II of this book to differentiate your brand and build trust with patrons.

APPENDIX C

Great Ideas for Building E-mail Lists

1. Sign-up form

The basic building block of your e-mail acquisition campaign should be a sign-up form that collects both e-mail address and postal-address information.

Be consistent. The same form should be presented to your patrons both online and offline, and you should collect the same information from each new patron. You want to ensure that you develop a consistent database of information.

When collecting e-mail addresses, your goal should be to also gather information about their interests at the same time. This will give you the opportunity to make your messages to them more relevant, since you'll be able to send targeted e-mails based on these interests.

Collecting basic information such as what genres of the arts most interest them or whether they have children living at home makes sense. Because each organization is different, we recommend you include questions that elicit just the information you need to market most effectively, based on your organization's activities. We've found patrons will willingly answer about four to five questions when they sign up.

Be careful not to confuse this sign-up form with a survey. If you need demographic information about your audience, survey later. (Online surveys are fast, inexpensive, and work extremely well.) For now, just ask for the specific information that will be relevant to your marketing.

2. Your site

Your website should be central to your e-mail acquisition campaign and a permanent feature of your ongoing list-building efforts. Here is a set of guidelines on design and placement that should improve your results.

Sign-up form pop-ups: Very few of your patrons come to your site specifically to sign up for your newsletter. The biggest percentage of visitors to arts sites are looking for time and date information about events or exhibitions.

Thus, getting someone to sign up on your site means interrupting their attention and motivating them to do something other than obtain the information they came there for in the first place.

To avoid frustration, we advocate employing a small screen that pops up when a user clicks a clearly defined link such as "Click here to sign up." Far from being an annoyance, a pop-up screen allows that person to stop what they are doing for a moment, fill out your form, and return to where they left off without feeling lost.

Home page: If you are familiar with your web traffic, you probably know that you're getting only a handful of page views from any given visitor. If you only get one or two clicks from each visitor, what are they going to click on first? If you make the sign-up form the most important link on the main page, you'll have more of a chance to get visitors to click on it.

Interior placements: In addition to your homepage, you should put your e-mail sign-up link in your navigation and add links on as many pages as possible. If you look at our site, www.patrontechnology.com, you'll see that the "Free Newsletters" link is persistent on every page.

3. Parking lot

You have three opportunities to reach people in your parking lot.

Upon arrival: If your lot has live attendants, your best approach would be to arrange to have the attendants hand out a sign-up card to be returned to them or turned in at the lobby. Offer an incentive, such as a discount on future parking, a discount ticket for the next event, or an intermission coffee.

Upon departure: If the form is returned at the garage (perhaps as patrons are paying), the attendant can hand the patron a coupon as the incentive. Ideally, the patron could even get an instant discount off the parking fee.

In some venues, there's a long line waiting to pay at the exit after the event. (If you've ever been to Tanglewood in the summer, you know that getting out of the free parking lot often takes a half-hour.) You can use this opportunity to have your volunteers walk up to cars that are waiting to pay and ask for sign-ups. (Clearly this is easier in more temperate climates.)

During the event: If the parking lot is automated, the windshield is a very useful place. During the event, have volunteers put a sign-up card under the wiper. The card should clearly spell out the benefit (and/or discount) for returning it upon exiting. Have a volunteer stationed there at the end of the performance collecting these forms.

4. Box office queue

Where there is a box office, there's usually a line. Why not convert this negative into a positive?

Station volunteers with clipboards and pencils and ask people to fill out the form while they wait in line. If we've learned anything from crowd control techniques at Disney theme parks, it's that diverting the attention of people who are waiting in line improves their overall perception of the experience.

Here's a moment to offer an incentive, such as, "If you fill this out today, we'll give you an instant $1 off your ticket purchase." If they are buying right away, they get the discount. If they are merely picking up tickets when they fill out the form, give them a coupon that is valid the next time they buy.

5. Coat check

The coat check is another offbeat place to solicit e-mail addresses. The attendants can give the sign-up form to patrons at the same time they give them their coats. Then, if there's a charge for the coat check, waive the charge if they fill out the form when they pick up their coats. Or offer some other discount or benefit if they return the card. Also, since coat-check lines tend to be long after an event, have a volunteer "work the line" by handing out sign-up cards while people are waiting in line.

6. Gift shop

Your gift shop is a good place to collect names because it's a place where your patrons tend to browse casually. Generally, the check-out line isn't as frantic as a box office line, and the sales staff can help do some one-on-one soliciting.

Make sure that the sign-up cards are in plain view in different areas of the store so that the casual shopper has several opportunities to encounter them. Don't forget to have plenty of golf pencils around or a pen attached to the table, similar to what you see at the bank.

7. Create retail partnerships

In many communities there are plenty of "arts-friendly" retail establishments with which to partner. You know which restaurants, cafes, and stores attract your patrons.

The potential of this idea first hit Gene when he visited Pittsburgh and walked around the arts district. Since there are several restaurants within walking distance of most of the arts venues, it seemed that these ought to be logical partners. After all, they are greeting a large number of your patrons just before they enter your venue. (This is even more true of restaurants that are located within your arts complex or hall.)

Offer local restaurants free promotional space in your e-mail newsletter in return for their cooperation in collecting e-mail names on your behalf. Then it's in their best interest to help you: The more names you have, the more people they reach.

You can use the same approach with local bookstores, gift shops, music stores, cafés, and coffee shops. Just pick stores that you believe your patrons will frequent and be creative about how you could leverage to your benefit their access to your patrons.

8. Online ticketing process

Perhaps the most logical place to secure an e-mail address is during the online ticketing process itself. As we learned from the FTC, it is legal to take the e-mail addresses supplied to you during the ticket-purchasing process and add them your e-mail list, so long as you comply with the editorial restrictions mandated by the CAN-SPAM law.

However, a far better way would be to apply the best business-practice approach by creating an opt-in section as part of the ticket-buying process. It need not be more complicated than adding a checkbox on the ticket-purchase screen:

> Please add me to your e-mail newsletter list so I can learn about future events, discounts, and special offers.

If you're using a third-party ticket vendor, you should contact them to add this to their online purchasing process, and then make sure you regularly receive those collected addresses.

Similarly, you should add this type of opt-in checkbox to all online forms you use to connect with your patrons, including online event registration, donations, and other solicitations. Make the collection of e-mail names part of every interactive process that your patrons engage in on your site.

9. List and message swapping

In addition to building your own list, you can also get your message out to potential patrons by collaborating with fellow arts institutions. The two primary ways are list swapping and message swapping.

List swapping: Many organizations have privacy policies that prohibit the sale or trade of their e-mail lists. (The proliferation of spam has created a protective culture regarding the sharing of e-mail information, which stands in stark contrast to the way that arts postal addresses are freely traded.) Many patrons won't sign up for a list that doesn't have this policy, so don't be surprised if you find this option limited.

As we said in Appendix B, if you can swap a list, you are required by CAN-SPAM to first match that borrowed list against your own list and remove any duplicates or opt-outs. If someone has opted out of your list, you cannot mail them again just because you borrowed their name from another organization.

Message swapping: A far easier approach is to swap messages with fellow arts organizations. The premise here is that you promote each other's events to your respective audiences in your own newsletters. You either create a solo mailing to your audience or include a message promoting another organization's event within your mailing. They then return the favor by doing the same for you.

This approach can have multiple benefits for both sides. Imagine sending an e-mail that says: "Because you're a valued patron of the Laboratory Theatre, we thought you'd like this special offer from our friends across town at the Drama Center. Here's a 20% discount for their current show, which runs through the end of this month, offered exclusively to you, our best patrons."

You've helped yourself in two ways. You've increased the value to your patrons by offering benefits they couldn't get elsewhere, and you've traded for the ability to promote your event to a new audience in the other organization's newsletter.

What's most important here is that the offer from the other organization be substantive. If you're merely promoting an event and there's nothing "in it" for your patrons, the message might be seen as a spam-like intrusion. So make sure you are delivering value, and use this as a negotiating tactic when you speak with your colleagues.

If your list sizes aren't exactly the same, swap e-mail names based on quantity. In other words, if you mail a message from the Civic Light Orchestra to your list of 10,000 names, and they have only 5,000 names, then you get two mailings to their audience for your single mailing.

Our clients who have tried this approach report that it has worked well.

10. Staff e-mail

Did you ever stop to wonder how many individual e-mails are sent collectively by you and your staff in a given month? We'll bet when you add up that number, it's impressive.

Use your staff e-mail as a place to encourage sign-ups. After all, the people you're writing to have some connection to your organization, so whether they are vendors or board members, they should be on your e-mail list.

Create an institution-wide footer for all e-mail that goes out from every employee for the duration of your campaign.

11. Thinking big: Community-wide e-mail list solicitation

Here's a bonus idea. Gene has pitched this idea many times before, but we don't think anyone has actually implemented it. So, we present it here as a challenge to the arts community at large.

Too often, arts marketers see each other as "competition" and apply a "for-profit" mentality to that word. The notion is that "if John and Sue buy a ticket to your event, that's one fewer ticket they will buy to my event." Or, "if John and Sue go to the other museum, they won't attend my exhibition."

We won't get into the accumulated research that dispels this myth, but most savvy marketers know that the real competition for arts patrons' time isn't other arts organizations at all. The competition is television, dinners out, children, travel, etc.

The most savvy and committed patrons attend lots of arts events. If you present them with something compelling, they will trade away a non-arts event for an arts event. Thus the "pie" for arts attendance isn't a fixed size. It can and will grow—based on effective marketing.

If indeed collecting arts patrons' information is a major challenge in each community, and if e-mail addresses are something that will be an asset for years to come, why not create a community-wide arts e-mail list acquisition campaign?

Take all the concepts that have been laid out above, and merely replicate them in a unified campaign with as many arts organizations as possible participating.

Make the campaign a community-wide event—get the local newspaper, a sponsor, and maybe even a foundation to help underwrite it. Create a unified sign-up form asking for people's interests with all the arts organizations' logos on the top. Explain to the patrons that this is a community-wide arts program for which they will be offered benefits and discounts unavailable to the general public. Enlist the support of a sponsor and enlist the support of all of your local media. Once completed, each arts organization would have access to the e-mails of all those people who indicated an interest in their genre.

We firmly believe that the power of doing this collaboratively would motivate arts patrons and leverage a common message that would achieve greater results than any single arts organization could get on its own.